Self-made

Self-made

by CAROL PINE and SUSAN MUNDALE

The Stories of 12 Minnesota Entrepreneurs.

DORN BOOKS
A Division of Dorn Communications, Inc.
Minneapolis

Copyright © 1982 by Dorn Books

Published by Dorn Books,
a division of Dorn Communications, Inc.,
7831 E. Bush Lake Rd., Minneapolis, MN 55435

Book design by Sara Christensen

Printed in the United States of America

ISBN 0-934070-11-3

Our thanks go to the many people whose help made this book possible, particularly researcher Deborah Gelbach, typist Dianne Amos and our editor, William Swanson.

Thanks also to these observers of the Minnesota business community: Don Larson, Dick Youngblood, John Borchert, D.M. Winton, Donald Soukup, Charles Mundale, Thomas O'Connell, David Speer, John "Jack" Robinson and Harold Chucker.

Thanks, too, to the many business associates, friends and family members of these 12 entrepreneurs. Their insights and recollections were invaluable in developing this book. A special thanks to the entrepreneurs themselves— for their time, their interest and their thoughts given through many hours of interviews.

This book is dedicated to the next generation of Minnesota entrepreneurs.

Contents

Introduction

A street-smart kid from Spanish Harlem bets on a "better" pacemaker.

A rookie salesman for Procter & Gamble bets on trading stamps.

A farm boy in western Minnesota bets on turkeys.

A feisty engineer bets on a new computer.

A Minneapolis housewife bets on pizza.

A miner's son from the Iron Range bets on bean sprouts.

These Minnesotans—and six others who have placed similar bets—are the subject of this book. All 12 are entrepreneurs and thus, by definition, risk-takers. They have wagered their savings, their property, their energy and their spirit for the sake of an idea. They have bet it all, and they have won.

To be an entrepreneur is to attempt to fulfill the American dream of individual achievement, wealth and power. Many are drawn to that dream. Every year, the number of newly organized corporations increases. So, alas, does the number of business failures. For those who succeed, the rewards are great. For those who fail, there are but two choices: give up or try again. Entrepreneurs seldom give up.

Why a book about *Minnesota* entrepreneurs? Certain regions of the United States seem to provide more fertile ground for the growth of new enterprise than others. Minnesota has been one of them. Consider the number of multimillion-dollar and multinational corporations "born and raised" in Minnesota in the late 19th and early 20th centuries: Minnesota Mining & Manufacturing, Honeywell, Pillsbury, Burlington Northern, General Mills, Cargill, Economics Laboratory, Dayton Hudson Corporation, Land O'Lakes, Farmers Union Central Exchange, Munsingwear, Weyerhaeuser Corporation. At one time, each of these mighty enterprises was nothing more than the kernel of an idea in the mind of an entrepreneur.

Today's business lore suggests that Minnesota produces more entrepreneurs per capita than most other states in the Union, though there are as yet no hard facts to substantiate that claim. National magazines single out Minnesota as a healthy state for entrepreneurship. Minnesota attracts high-technology companies, they say, because civic and governmental leaders have been sensitive to the needs of small business. They also credit proximity to the University of Minnesota, as well as the state's high regard for education at all levels. Furthermore, Minnesota abounds with venture capitalists and investors who have also been willing to place bets on fresh ideas.

"In Minnesota local entrepreneurship may well be even more necessary for local job creation than it is in some other parts of the United States," says University of Minnesota professor and geographer John R. Borchert in his 1975 study, *Entrepreneurship and Future Employment in Minnesota.* "This region has always lacked important resources of energy; it is on the geographical margin of the national market; and it is not a geographical concentration of low-priced labor. Circumstances would seem to demand that people within the state invent ways to serve the national and local markets and thus to create jobs that otherwise would not exist here."

Whatever the factors, the success rate of Minnesota entrepreneurs may be better than average. Many of the early state-based ventures have turned out to be major market forces, and the enterprises described in this book are themselves now significant players in the world market-place. Among them are Control Data and Medtronic, the Carlson Companies and Jeno's, Inc. All 12 were once-small companies that took hold and grew large in fertile Minnesota.

The 12 entrepreneurs profiled in this book are not, by any means, the only entrepreneurs active in Minnesota. These particular entrepreneurs, however, represent a span of generations, a variety of ethnic and geographical origins, a range of industries and a diversity of personalities. Some are well-known Minnesotans who established their empires in the 1940s and 1950s; some are not so well-known and more recent arrivals. Some have founded a series of companies; for them, the challenge has been in developing a product and bringing it to market, not in maintaining the momentum for years afterward. Some, on the other hand, have developed a single corporation and become full-fledged managers in their own right. And it is no accident, by the way, that this selection of entrepreneurs includes several involved in high technology and food processing: Both are major Minnesota industries with a rich history of entrepreneurship.

To attempt a "definitive" list of Minnesota entrepreneurs with absorbing stories would be, inevitably, to omit significant names. Instead, we offer the profiles of the following dozen, convinced that their experiences, taken together, are representative of the most fascinating, and perhaps the most important, phenomenon in the business world.

☐ Of course, it would be hazardous to generalize about *all* entrepreneurs from the stories of just a dozen. But through months of interviews with these 12, their families and associates, we have discovered enough similarities to convince us that successful entrepreneurs share a number of important qualities.

The entrepreneurs in this book seem to be either product-oriented "inventors" or market-oriented "salesmen." The inventors were tinkerers even as children. Their forte as adults has been creating new products to fill niches in the market—niches that at first only they can see. The salesmen have taken existing products and created new and bigger markets.

Product-oriented inventors often begin in basement or garage workshops, but they set their sights high. G.T. Schjeldahl invented bag-making machines for polyethylene even before "plastics" became a buzz word—and he saw beyond his workbench to future markets. Earl Bakken's laboratory yielded a medical device that could save thousands of lives—and he knew enough about cardiac treatment to turn that device into an implantable pacemaker. Market-oriented entrepreneurs create sales networks and expand them with innovation and imagination. Curt Carlson started with a "sleeper"—trading stamps—and sold them with more gusto and to more customers than anyone else. Earl Olson, Marvin Schwan and Rose Totino took food products they grew up with—turkey, ice cream and pizza—and created businesses with markets well beyond the neighborhood restaurant or corner grocery.

Not one of the 12 in this book comes from a background of wealth. Four are the children of immigrants. Several are the grandchildren of Midwest homesteaders. From their parents and grandparents they inherited a fundamental faith in individual effort. Jeno Paulucci's mother opened a grocery store in the Paulucci home during the Depression. Marvin Schwan's parents, in middle age, invested their life savings in a dairy partnership. G.T. Schjeldahl's mother used her skill as a seamstress to build a ladies' tailoring business. Richard Schaak's father founded his own neighborhood electronics business. Curt Carlson's father bought a corner grocery store, and his mother opened her own bakery. William Norris' father and grandfather were Nebraska farmers. Dean Scheff's father bought a country elevator and dabbled in commodities futures. Earl Olson's father traded horses and finally scraped together enough money to buy a farm in western Minnesota. Each child grew up with a strong sense of self and a powerful ego that could withstand criticism and doubt. As adults, they would not be denied.

Every one of these entrepreneurs started early. At an age when most children were playing sand-lot baseball or make-believe, these 12 were already involved in what would become their life's work. Some were already turning a profit. Curt Carlson organized his siblings in a newspaper sales network before he was 10. At about the same age, Jeno Paulucci was selling vials of iron-ore samples to

Iron Range tourists. Young Earl Bakken built a functioning robot in his family's basement. Lou Cosentino could dissect and reassemble any household appliance before he was 15. Richard Schaak made and sold bows and arrows to archers on the tournament circuit. William Norris trapped squirrels, sold the skins, and used his earnings to buy electronic gadgets. Dean Scheff sold garden seed and "magic" salve to any warm body he could find in Lime Creek, Minnesota.

For several of them—particularly the children of the Depression—jobs were a necessity, and their earnings were part of the family income. Rose Totino peddled milk from the family cow to neighbors in northeast Minneapolis. From his early teens, Paulucci contributed cash to the household coffers and helped send his sister to school. Earl Olson became a farmhand at the age of six.

All 12, not surprisingly, were recognized as bright, sometimes precocious children. But not all of them did well in school. Schjeldahl found his classroom studies boring. Schaak dropped out of college and electronics school. Scheff was slow learning how to read, and teachers considered him flippant or worse. Of the 12, only five completed college, and only one, Cosentino, earned an advanced degree. All 12 have continued to educate themselves, however, through reading and ceaseless on-the-job learning. They have all made the world their classroom.

One quality definitely shared by these and other entrepreneurs is the ability to focus intense energy and thought on one idea over long periods of time. They have not been distracted by the environment. Instead, the environment has fueled their imaginations, yielding new ideas and new approaches. They have, moreover, demonstrated a great —often single-minded—drive to succeed. Drive implies discipline, fortitude and toughness—three characteristics frequently cited by their associates. They have shown a fundamental need to control their lives and the conditions around them. Most began their careers as employees in an uncomfortable but necessary apprenticeship. They were dissatisfied in large corporations, chiefly because they felt inadequately rewarded. They created, and their creations often died of neglect; or they sold more goods than any of their corporate peers, and were rewarded with a gold watch or less. They were square pegs that would not fit the round holes of corporate bureaucracy. They were, in a sense, "unemployable."

To reject the corporate life meant risk, but entrepreneurs have always had a unique view of risk. For them, it is hardly risk at all. They are so convinced of the rightness of their ideas that they scarcely consider failure as a possibility. For them, risk is an opportunity, not a threat. If they do fail, they start over. Like most entrepreneurs, these 12 have had an uncommon faith in themselves. They haven't required evidence of support from others. What has mattered is not what others have thought of them, but what they have thought of themselves.

□ Some years ago, psychologists identified two styles of thinking—convergent (rational and systematic) and divergent (thinking that branches off, often in several directions at once). Most scientists think convergently, eliminating errors and solving problems through a systematic process of elimination. Divergent thinking, on the other hand, leads to unpredictable conclusions, fresh associations and the elusive "aha!" Entrepreneurs are generally divergent thinkers, eschewing traditional solutions. For them, "It's always been done this way" is meaningless, and "It can't be done" is a challenge.

"The essential characteristics of entrepreneurial activity are obvious in some ways, yet in other ways are as elusive as the spark of creativity itself," says Professor Borchert. He describes, for example, the entrepreneur's response to information:

"Like all the rest of us, an entrepreneur in action is responding to information about the needs and resources around him in society. But his or her response is a more complex, a more nearly unique response. He uses more information than most other people, or he uses it more quickly, or both. He creates a new or critically modified institutional structure rather than simply working within an organization as he finds it. His use of information probably requires more work and more risk than that of people less involved in organizing and reorganizing the resources of nature and man. Entrepreneurs are key nodes in the ever-spreading, intensifying international network of management, financial, and personnel information."

Successful entrepreneurs know their own industries.

They have a keen sense of timing and an accurate feel for current markets. But they can also see beyond present trends. "When G.T. Schjeldahl first came to us with his ideas for polyethylene-packaging machines," says venture capitalist John Robinson, "there was only enough polyethylene in the world for 20 machines." When Manny Villafana founded St. Jude Medical to manufacture heart valves, he was told he had entered a shrinking industry. When Bill Norris instructed his staff to build peripherals to serve Control Data's computers and then sold those peripherals to competing companies, critics said he was cutting his own throat. When Dick Schaak decided to court a market larger than radio repairmen and ham radio enthusiasts, observers merely shook their heads. And when Rose Totino and her husband Jim opened a restaurant in 1951, pizza was virtually unheard of in Minnesota. All saw beyond the bounds of traditional markets.

Entrepreneurs are decisive. They like to act quickly and unilaterally. These 12 are not team players; many once had partners who eventually left or were forced out. If they chose to collaborate at all, it was during the early stages when collaboration was essential for survival. Later on, however, collaboration gave way to singular control. "Partnership," Bill Norris scoffs. "That only works for lawyers and accountants!"

But as their organizations grew, these entrepreneurs faced compelling adjustments. Their inherent need to control eventually gave way to management structure, to delegation and to thoughts of succession. How these 12 handled that issue is a fascinating aspect of their stories. For some, letting go has been difficult and painful—and, in some cases, impossible. Others have made costly mistakes, bringing in accommodating people who were, in effect, "yes men" functioning as the entrepreneur's mirror image. After a few false starts, some of the entrepreneurs began building organizations with persons who had the skills they lacked. "The more weaknesses I recognize, the stronger I become," Schjeldahl says now.

Monetary reward has been one incentive for these entrepreneurs, but it has not always been primary. Money has, for most of them, been a symbol of recognition for what they have accomplished and the means to accomplish more. Ironically, while successful entrepreneurship can

lead to great wealth, almost all of the 12 have been too pre-
occupied with their businesses to spend that wealth
lavishly. Rose Totino, for instance, is still content in the
home she and her husband bought in the mid-1940s. Only
recently did Bill Norris move away from the middle-class
St. Paul neighborhood he called home for many years. In
this state of purposeful reserve, Curt Carlson may be the
most lavish of them all. But even Carlson doesn't have a
chauffeur, and he still pumps his own gas.

At the same time, there seems to be an unwritten rule of
behavior in Minnesota that compels the self-made man or
woman to give something back to society. Paulucci has
tirelessly crusaded to improve the economy of northeastern
Minnesota. Norris has supported entrepreneurial efforts in
dozens of creative ways. Totino was among the original
"five percenters," giving five percent of her company's
pre-tax profits to support community programs and charitable organizations. Schwan has endowed a "Free Enterprise Chair" at Southwest State University in his
hometown of Marshall. Bakken has created a library and
museum devoted to the study of electricity in life.

Entrepreneurs make other contributions as well, and
chief among them is jobs. "New companies have become a
vital source of American economic growth," says *Time*
magazine in a recent article entitled *Striking It Rich*. "According to Stanley Pratt, editor of the *Venture Capital
Journal,* small businesses created three million jobs in the
past 10 years. The largest 1,000 American firms, on the
other hand, recorded virtually no net gain in employment
during the same period."

All in all, entrepreneurs are still the key figures in the
vitality of American business. "They give such a gift,"
says one Minnesota-based venture capitalist who has
financed many new companies. "The things they do are
bold and audacious and can result in real changes in our
systems and materials. They do what they do out of com-
pulsion; they seem to have no choice. But what they give is
so great, and their positive impact is extraordinary. They
inspire people to see potential in new ideas, and their bold
acts inspire risk-taking in others."

But because of the intense dedication to their ventures,
entrepreneurs risk becoming one-dimensional. "At a party," says a venture capitalist, "they are the dullest folks.

They don't mix well, and they have no patience for small talk." "They are the opposite of Renaissance men," says another observer. A few of these entrepreneurs have made an effort to broaden their lives—but only *after* their business success has been assured. Few take vacations; few have hobbies. When they do play, they tend to play with the same intensity they show in their work.

Still, they are having a wonderful time. They are not workoholics—if workoholics are people who spend long hours on the job but would rather be somewhere else. These entrepreneurs enjoy their work because work is their lives. Retirement is unimaginable; they will probably be active until the end. For them, entrepreneurship is the only game in town.

Jeno Paulucci

1

Jeno Paulucci

The Kid with the Argentine Bananas

It is the mid-1920s. An Italian family in Hibbing, Minnesota, is dressed in its Sunday best to pose for a family portrait. The father, stiffly uncomfortable in a double-breasted suit and bow tie, his hair parted squarely down the middle and clipped high above his ears, gazes into the distance behind the camera. His older child, a girl, wears a fashionable dress and a long string of pearls. She carries a violin and bow—our clue to the occasion frozen in memory by the photograph.

The mother, sternly unsmiling, holds a new patent-leather purse in one hand. Her other hand rests on the shoulder of her only son. Dressed in a scaled-down version of his father's suit, his shoes shined and his curly hair barely tamed, the boy looks squarely at us. He has a smile on his face and a look in his eye you swear is a challenge. This is a kid to be reckoned with, one who will make his mark on the world.

The boy is Luigino Francesco Paulucci, the Italian immigrant's son who will, as all Minnesotans know, make a fortune selling canned Chinese food to American housewives from unlikely headquarters in northern Minnesota. This is the entrepreneur who will eventually sell his Chinese-food company, Chun King, for $63 million (giving $2 million to its employees), then turn his attention to a stepchild operation called Northland Foods, rename it and make it the number-one pizza-maker in the country. This is a boy who will find his trademark at 10 when he renames himself "Jeno"—with an extra flourish on the J. To Minnesotans, he is not "Mr. Paulucci," he is *Jeno*. And he needs no further identification.

☐ During his childhood, Jeno Paulucci was poor even by Depression standards. His father, Ettore, had migrated to Aurora, Minnesota, to work in the iron mines. But work was irregular and money scarce, and the family had to scrounge to keep food on the table. In Aurora, Ettore earned $4.20 for a 13-hour day—when he could get work. The Pauluccis shared a $5-a-month, four-room flat with scurrying insects, later the basis for Jeno's "cockroach theory" of customer complaints: "If you see one, there must be 100 more you don't know about."

When mining jobs dwindled, Ettore tried others. He kept a job as janitor in the public school by serving local officials free plates of his wife's homemade spaghetti and illegally brewed wine. ("My first experience with cheap, miserable grafters," Jeno would later write in his autobiography, *How It Was To Make $100,000,000 in a Hurry*.) Everyone in the family pitched in. Young Jeno gleaned the railroad tracks for fallen lumps of coal, pulling a little red wagon he'd made of discarded parts. He gathered cardboard boxes to sell—for a penny each—to the landlord who burned them for fuel in the four-flat building the Pauluccis called home.

In the early 1920s, the family moved to Hibbing, and Ettore went back to the mines. But eventually the Depression made employment even more intermittent than it had been in Aurora. Ettore and Michelina expanded their wine-making operation. Jeno and his sister Liz helped out by chopping creosote-soaked roadbed timbers for firewood. Michelina catered dinner parties with steaming Italian food prepared in her kitchen and delivered in a wagon pulled by Liz and Jeno. On Saturdays, Jeno unloaded coal at a lumberyard for $1 a car and whatever scraps he could carry home.

Clearly, Jeno Paulucci was no stranger to hard work. But early on, he realized he had more than the muscle he'd developed shoveling coal. He began figuring other ways to make a buck. He gathered horse manure at one lumber-yard and sold it to the owner of another for garden fer-tilizer. He peddled iron-ore samples in glass vials to tourists who came to see the Mahoning pit outside Hibb-ing, and he served as an enthusiastic guide when they wanted to venture into abandoned mine shafts in the neighborhood. He was not yet 12 years old.

Though short of money, the Pauluccis did not lack in resourcefulness. When the mining company offered to sell abandoned houses near the north Hibbing ore pits for $125 each (presumably for firewood) the family bought one and had it moved to a lot they managed to buy in the south part of town. Jeno, Liz and Michelina made the foundation themselves out of old telephone poles. When a truck went out to put up new poles, they followed in their 1929 Ford, tying a rope around the old ones and dragging them, one by one, to their construction site, where Jeno and his mother cut them to size.

In 1933, Michelina Paulucci opened a neighborhood grocery in the living room of that clapboard house in south Hibbing. As usual, it was a family affair. Among other assignments, Liz and Jeno had to decide what kinds of penny candy the store would carry. In any other family, the reward might have been unlimited dipping into the bar-rel. Not in Jeno's. He decreed that the two of them would be allowed no more than three cents' worth of candy— *retail*—per day. The idea, Jeno knew, was to *sell* the candy and make money, not to eat up the profits.

By the age of 14, Jeno had his first regular job at Hibbing's Downtown Daylight Market. He scurried up and down stairs from storeroom to grocery shelves before school, after school and all day Saturday from 5 a.m. to midnight. He became locally famous, he says, for "run-ning around with one 50-pound sack of flour or sugar on my shoulder and another under my arm and in general be-ing a very eager beaver."

The Downtown Daylight Market was one of a chain owned by David Persha, who lived 70 miles away in Duluth. Persha remembers driving to Hibbing to see firsthand this teenaged dynamo his brother, the store's manager, had hired. Persha also wanted to check on the carload of strawberries he had shipped to Hibbing late in the season.

What he saw amazed him. Here was this kid telling a rapt audience of housewives—in Italian—that it was their last chance to buy strawberries, that his mother had reserved 10 cases, and with only a few cases left, they'd better buy theirs right away. What's more, Persha noted, Jeno had boosted the price!

"How much you paying this kid?" Persha asked his brother.

"Fifty cents a day, plus some meat to take home," the manager replied.

"You'd better put him on the regular payroll and give him as much as the other clerks."

"Whenever I had a carload of merchandise," Persha recalls, "I'd say, 'Jeno, get this sold.' Jeno worked his head off."

It was the beginning of a long and sometimes stormy friendship. Jeno was temperamental, and the other clerks were jealous of both his ability to sell and his status with Persha. "We were like father and son," says Persha. " 'That your boy?' strangers would ask. 'That's my boy,' I'd say. 'But sometimes I'd like to disown him!' " (Jeno's own father, a soft-spoken, gentle man, drifted away from the family when his children grew older. They were not reunited until Jeno had a family of his own.)

That summer and summers afterward, Jeno served as troubleshooter for all Persha's stores in northeastern Minnesota. At 16, he became notorious as the youngest and loudest barker on Duluth's produce row. Fired by competition with the big kid in the fruit stand across the street, Jeno put everything he had into cajoling customers to buy Persha's fruit and vegetables.

Once, when Persha's refrigerator plant broke down and ammonia fumes blanketed the store's stock, Jeno turned disaster into opportunity. Seeing 18 crates of bananas that had turned an oily, speckled brown on the outside but were otherwise unharmed, Persha gave Jeno orders to get rid of the discolored fruit at bargain prices. Goaded by his smirking rival across the street, Jeno hand-lettered a sign— "Argentine Bananas"—and began extolling the virtues of this "exotic" fruit. A crowd gathered and within three hours Jeno had moved all 18 crates at *his* price: four cents a pound *higher* than the price of "ordinary" bananas.

Jeno took to merchandising as though he'd been born to it. "I'd start real early in the morning—maybe around six—and work until 11 or 12 at night," he says. "If I saw anybody within earshot, I'd holler. On Saturday night, I'd chase people up the street trying to sell a bushel of spinach for a quarter—because I knew by Monday it would be spoiled. My job was to clean up everything." For Jeno, it was more fun than splashing around in a country-club pool. "Whenever we had an oversupply of something, I had a 10-minute sale complete with an alarm clock and two clerks. I'd get up on a box so I could see the crowd and start hollering: 'For 10 minutes only, tomatoes four pounds for a dollar!' When the alarm clock rang and the sale was over, somebody in the crowd would ask, 'How much are they now?' 'Same price,' I'd say. People loved it. I found you can have fun doing anything."

The competition between Jeno and his adversary across the street grew white-hot that summer. "They even brought in an older kid to out-yell me," he remembers. Before long, a petition against the youthful pitchmen became a city ordinance against fruit-stand barking. It was the beginning of a lifelong love-hate relationship between Jeno and the city of Duluth. "I don't blame them," Jeno says in retrospect. "There were doctors and lawyers on the second floor of the building. How would you like to work up there with me barking all day right outside the window?"

It was quite a year. Jeno earned $16 a week that summer, spent $3 for a rented room and saved the rest. Sunday mornings, he thumbed a ride back to Hibbing to take care of his mother's store so she could go to the movies. Then, fortified with a good Italian meal, he caught the Tastee-Bread truck back to Duluth at midnight. During the school year he worked at the Downtown Daylight Market in Hibbing.

Despite the hectic schedule, Jeno was a quick, bright student. He even had time for extras: debate, writing for the school paper, acting in school plays. Then as now, he loved an argument, a cause. He led two strikes at Hibbing High: one against long homework assignments (unfair to kids who had jobs), the other against having to learn poetry, a discipline he considered completely without merit.

Graduating at 16, Jeno enrolled at Hibbing Junior College to study pre-law. He also kept his job at Persha's store, where his ability to move merchandise attracted the attention of visiting salesmen. Word reached the wholesale grocery firm of Hancock-Nelson in St. Paul, and Jeno got an offer to open the company's northern Minnesota sales territory and earn a percentage of the profits. There was one catch: Jeno would have to give up college.

It was a tough decision. "A good lawyer, I'd heard, might make $50,000 a year—quite a salary for 1937. But a good marketing man might make the world his oyster." He had obligations to think of, too, including his sister's education at the University of Minnesota. After some thought, Jeno quit school and signed on with one condition: he wanted exactly 50 percent of the profits. Hancock-Nelson agreed.

Barnstorming northern Minnesota and Wisconsin, Jeno slept in his car and ate on the run. He learned to sell carload lots to groups of grocers he'd encouraged to join forces for a volume discount. He set up "buy-by-the-case" promotions in local stores, and he used his fertile imagination. "Green Giant's peas are mixed sizes," he would say. "Not these—these peas are *all* big. None of those little peas mixed in here—and you can have them for only $1.25 a dozen cans."

Jeno turned out to be Hancock-Nelson's hottest salesman. So hot, in fact, that he made more money than the company's president. Hancock-Nelson insisted on changing the deal: Jeno would go on a straight salary with an undefined bonus. Jeno quit—but not before he'd invested $1,000 in a business venture of his own.

Calling on a Backus, Minnesota, grocery, he spied neatly packaged bags of dehydrated garlic selling from a display card for 10 cents each. The garlic had been brought in from California, he learned, by a man and wife vacationing nearby. Jeno found the Californian with 5,000 cards of garlic and came away with 100 for 50 cents a card. He added them to his wholesale route.

Before long, the garlic was sold, and Jeno made a pact with the Californian: all 5,000 cards for 20 cents each. When those cards were sold (at a 60-cent-per-card profit),

Jeno returned to the Californian, who "just happened" to have 5,000 additional cards. These cost Jeno 40 cents each, plus payments toward a dehydrating machine the Californian claimed he needed to supply more garlic.

"It was my first experience in getting conned good and clean," Jeno says. "I didn't know it, but you could buy the garlic, already dehydrated, in 25-pound drums from California. What's more, the guy was filling orders from my stores through another rep who paid him 20 cents more." Jeno began packaging his own garlic.

□ By the time he left Hancock-Nelson, Jeno had a sizeable wholesale garlic business. He retreated temporarily to Persha's Duluth store, working nights at a shipyard to fill his spare time. Every now and then, he took a few days off to sell garlic.

It was on one of those garlic-selling trips that Jeno discovered bean sprouts. He learned that Nisei in Minneapolis were growing them in hydroponic gardens, and that they couldn't keep up with the demand. It was wartime by now, and fresh vegetables were in short supply, so restaurants and grocers were buying the sprouts as fast as they were grown.

In the basement of Persha's store, Jeno punched holes in a tub and filled it with wet soybeans. Eager to get started, he didn't realize that the sprouts grew from a special kind of seed, the seed of mung beans. Soon the earthy odor from the soybeans ("like rotting potatoes") permeated Persha's store. With the garlic Jeno was packaging in the back room, the soybean fiasco was a test of Persha's friendship if there ever was one. But Persha was intrigued. He was ready to get out of the grocery business and look for something new. He and Jeno joined forces.

Jeno approached a Duluth bank for his first business loan. "I don't suppose I'll ever forget the look on the banker's face when I told him I wanted to borrow $2,500 to grow *bean sprouts* from *mung beans*," he wrote later. The banker said no, and Jeno turned to a family friend, food broker Antonio Papa, who granted the $2,500 loan. Jeno and Persha set up shop, and the enterprise grew quickly. Before long, semi-trailers were blocking traffic on First Street as they loaded aboard sprouts bound for Eastern markets.

As partners, Persha and Paulucci were an unlikely pair. Persha, an older man with the air of a continental gentleman, had been in business for years. He was reasonable and cautious. Jeno, younger and more impetuous, had wild ideas that sprang up faster than brush fires. A healthy competition grew between the two. They vied to see who would arrive at work first. "Then we'd go across the street at lunch to see who could eat the most sausage," Jeno reminisced later.

The partners sold their sprouts in bushel baskets to Eastern processors who were, Jeno says, "taking us for a ride." The processors claimed spoilage when Paulucci and Persha couldn't prove otherwise, then went ahead and resold the sprouts at full value. So Jeno decided they would can the sprouts themselves. Calling themselves the Bean Sprout Growers Association, the two men contacted the War Production Board in Washington and obtained a million "obsolete" cans that had small imperfections but posed no health problems. Then they found a rundown plant in Iron River, Wisconsin, and began canning their sprouts. Before long, they expanded the line, mixing celery and pimento with the sprouts to make chop suey vegetables and selling them under the "Foo Young" brand name.

Jeno scouted the country for bargains. He paid a penny per pound for celery branches that a Florida packing company was discarding. He bought slightly scratched metal cans for chow mein noodles. "It didn't affect the product at all, because chow mein noodles are dry," he recalls. "And I was able to pass on to the consumer a lower cost. Sometimes I say I built the business on rejects."

The year 1945 was one of change for Jeno. It was the year he stopped drinking. During his grocery-and-garlic sales career, he was known occasionally to hit a bar and, all too often, he wrote later, to "start hitting other patrons of the bar. I had more fights than anybody five-feet-five-inches tall has any business having."

The second floor above his bean-sprout operation housed the Greek Club, a popular Duluth nightspot. When Jeno drew night-watering duty, he made frequent visits to the club upstairs for a few drinks. "In between watering every four hours, what else was I to do?" he says.

"We had a little butcher shop in the front of the building, so one night, around midnight, I cut myself a steak and went into the back room to cook it. The next thing I knew, I was in jail. I guess I was caught chasing a man from Wisconsin with two butcher knives. That taught me to quit. I said, 'Jeno, drinking is not for you.' It wasn't such a tough thing. I just said to hell with it.''

Lois Trepanier might also have had something to do with his sudden reform. A vivacious and popular Duluth girl from the other side of the tracks (the *good* side, Jeno says), she had little in common with the cigar-smoking sprout-grower whose idea of a big date was to drive over to Iron River and check on his canning operation.

Lois worked at the Duluth, Missabi & Iron Range Railway. After months of watching her in the cafe where she took her coffee break, Jeno finally arranged an introduction through a friend they had in common. On their first date, he took her to the Greek Club, where he spent the evening alternately making attempts at conversation through a haze of cigar smoke and running downstairs to see if the beans were sprouting. "We didn't hit it off at all," Lois says. "He couldn't get me home fast enough."

Several months passed before Jeno called Lois for a second date—to take that drive to Wisconsin and the canning plant. This time, they got along better, and in September 1945 they became engaged. The couple set the date for June, but the anxious Jeno kept moving it up. On their wedding day, February 8, 1946, more bets were placed than on any marriage Duluth had ever seen. Lois came from a family of French and English heritage. The Trepaniers were reserved and relatively undemonstrative. Jeno was, well, Jeno.

Their first year was the toughest. For one thing, while Lois had enjoyed a busy social life, Jeno was used to turning in at 8 p.m. so he'd be fresh when he got up at 4 the next morning to go to the office. For another, the newly-weds were barely settled in their apartment when Persha and Paulucci were slapped with a lawsuit brought by their canner at Iron River, who claimed they had raised their prices without cutting him in. Jeno fought the case stubbornly, refusing to settle. The suit eventually cost the partners $64,000, plus legal and court fees of $18,000—an $82,000 lesson.

Then, to make matters worse, the Iron River cannery burned down. Discouraged but not beaten, Jeno found a former rutabaga-canning plant in Grand Rapids, Minnesota, and immediately converted it to handle bean sprouts. But the fire, Jeno's stubborn insistence on fighting the lawsuit and his various "wild" ideas finally proved more than Persha wanted to handle. They decided to part, with Jeno buying out Persha's half of the business.

It was 1947, and Jeno owed everybody money—his packers, his suppliers, even some of his customers who had credit memos. A federal investigator, moreover, determined that Paulucci owed his employees $15,000 in back pay for time-and-a-half over 40 hours instead of 48 as stated in their union contract. Jeno bid on a government contract to pack boned turkey on the basis of a verbal loan agreement from a Duluth bank. When the bank backed out, he had to tell the government to take the next lowest bid. Finally, a small Duluth bank granted him a loan.

In an effort to settle one debt, Jeno made an agreement with the packer who had won the lawsuit. Jeno would act as a field broker, selling the packer's canned pie fillings at a low brokerage rate. But the packer, who had been so prompt about collecting payments on the settlement, proved slow to pay the brokerage fee. Again Jeno took matters into his own hands. He telephoned the packer's company with a fictitious order for $9,000 worth of pie filling. When the cans were in the truck and on their way to Duluth, he phoned the packer again. "If I don't get $5,000 by tomorrow, I'm going to dump this stuff in the Twin Cities for bargain prices," he said. "Furthermore, I'm going into the pie-filling business myself, and it's a vendetta." Northland Foods, later Jeno's, Inc., was thus born.

That same year, Foo Young nearly lost its biggest account to the competition. To avert the disaster, Jeno proposed a head-to-head taste test in the buyer's office. Paulucci opened his canned vegetables first—and sitting right on the top was a fat, juicy, *cooked* grasshopper. Without batting an eye, Jeno exclaimed that the vegetables looked so good *he* would take the first bite. The grasshopper disappeared, the buyer never knew what had happened, and the account was saved. It was the first break Jeno had had in a long, long time.

Business began to brighten. Foo Young was renamed the Chun King Corporation. Michelina Paulucci was lured away from her grocery store in Hibbing to act as a product consultant, improving the bland Chinese vegetables with some judicious Italian seasonings and bolstering the chow mein noodles with the leavening she used in her castellioni. It was Chinese food with an Italian accent, and the customers loved it.

In 1951, Chun King opened a shiny new plant in working-class West Duluth. The company had a trucking subsidiary called Orient Express, as well as plans for celery farms and a variety of new products.

Duluth, of all places, became the chow-mein capital of the world, and for many years Jeno Paulucci meant to keep it that way. He insisted on strict quality control, enforcing it himself with taste samplings every two hours. He regularly overturned garbage cans to monitor waste. He invented the "Divider-Pak" (two cans taped together, one on top of the other) in a moment of inspiration after mulling over the problem of mushy vegetables in the meat sauce.

The company eventually began to attract acquisition offers. One came from a syndicate of Duluth businessmen, including an attorney who had once turned down Jeno's offer to sell him half the company for $25,000. The syndicate offered a couple hundred thousand. "We just turned down Chef Boy-Ar-Dee," Paulucci replied, "and they offered $4 million."

How did Jeno know when it was time to sell? "I went through a little ritual every morning. I would say to myself, 'Jeno, you just sold Chun King. How do you feel?' For years the answer was, 'Terrible.' When the answer changed to, 'Great,' I knew it was time to sell."

On November 28, 1966, Paulucci finally sold Chun King to R.J. Reynolds Tobacco Company for $63 million. Chun King would be part of a new division called Reynolds Foods, and Jeno would be chairman of the Reynolds Foods board, working one week a month at Reynolds headquarters in New York. Ironically, it would not be a "great" arrangement for Jeno.

When he showed up for work at his usual time the first morning, the guard wouldn't let him into the building. "I suddenly realized that I was in a different world!" he says. "These people came to work at *nine* in the morning. I thought I was late walking in at *six*!" It was an education in the workings of a large corporation, and, not surprisingly, Jeno found it not to his liking. In three years he resigned. He had his eyes on another venture.

Reynolds, it seems, had agreed that if any Chun King employees were unhappy, they could go back to work for Jeno. And the parent company agreed to pack pizza rolls—Jeno's new venture—at cost plus five percent. The popularity of both egg rolls and pizza suggested to Paulucci that there might be a market for a *new* snack—pizza rolls.

"Reynolds never did ask me what a pizza roll was," Paulucci chuckles. "Three or four months after the sale, I told them I needed 50,000 cases of pizza rolls, and they almost went into shock.

" 'How are we going to get the equipment?' they asked me.

" 'You already have the equipment—pizza rolls are nothing but egg rolls with pizza crust and filling,' I said.

"They've been upset with me ever since. They thought I pulled a fast one on them, and actually it was their own ignorance."

Paulucci poured the cash from the Chun King sale into other business ventures, including stodgy Northland Foods, now Jeno's, Inc. But first, he distributed $2 million among his Chun King employees. "If any of them had ever wanted to start their own business, they now had the capital to get started," he says. It was also his way of thanking them, he later said, "for not bugging me about a goddamn bowling team."

In the next 10 years, a dizzying array of new products with Jeno's bright label joined the pizza rolls in frozen-food cases across the land. By 1979, when Jeno stepped down and his son Michael took over as chairman, the company had revenues of more than $150 million. But Jeno's, Inc., slipped behind Pillsbury's Totino brand as the number-one pizza-maker in the country, a situation Jeno, now a consultant, refused to tolerate.

By the end of 1981, the pizza battle raged on several fronts. Jeno's was spending more on advertisements than Totino's ($8 million to $6 million). Jeno's filed suit against Pillsbury, charging that Totino's "Crisp Crust" patent was stolen from Jeno's. Pillsbury filed a suit alleging that Jeno's, Inc., had engaged in unfair competition by packaging pizza in a container that "simulates Totino's packaging." In January 1982, attorneys for Jeno's sent letters to 3,000 television stations around the country asking them not to run some Totino's commercials on the grounds that they contained false and deceptive statements.

Jeno has never been one to pull or duck any punches.

□ Jeno's story has been told many times. Some of that story is the stuff of legend, and this five-foot-five, Italian miner's son is as well-known in the North Country as the larger but less feisty Paul Bunyan. "You can love him or hate him," an associate once told a reporter, "but you can no more deny him than you can deny a gale-force wind on Lake Superior."

Though now in his mid-60s, he still arrives at his rambling, nondescript Duluth headquarters no later than 6:30 in the morning. The telephone is his link to the world. "When I get to the office, I think, 'Where can I start?' First, I call people in Italy or England or Germany because they're seven hours ahead of us. Then I work backward to New York and the rest of the U.S." When he leaves the office at 5 p.m., it's only the "official" end of his work day. Jeno never really stops. Watching television at home, he makes notes with an ever-present pencil and pad. "He's thinking all the time," says Lois.

He works part of Saturday and sometimes goes to the office on Sunday "just to genuflect." "Actually," he says, "I think there's plenty of time in the work week. Lunch—two eggs, four eggs, depends on how hungry I am—takes one minute, where if I went out and sat with the guys and waited for the waitress it would take two hours. I use my time for what I want to do, and I have plenty of time to get everything done."

Some credit for Jeno's efficiency goes to his secretary, Gail Bukowski, who has occupied her post just outside his office since 1955. ("He's a wild man—you won't last a week," her former boss said when Paulucci hired her.) "With Jeno, there's no such thing as hold," she says. Whether he is in Italy, in Florida or 30 feet away in his office, her job is the same: to respond immediately if not sooner.

Jeno does not use a tape recorder; he dictates in person or over the phone. His letters have the immediacy—and the language—of Jeno in the flesh. Nothing sits long on his desk, suggesting one of his several axioms: "Do it, and do it *now*."

"I would rather be working seven days a week than playing golf or cards or going to ballgames or whatever," he explains. "The world of sports included, there's just no better game than being an entrepreneur. It's like climbing the highest mountain over and over again with the same type of exhilaration each time.

"An entrepreneur has to be damn near a workoholic," he continues. "You have to know how to discipline yourself, to communicate and control. At times you have to be devious—I don't mean dishonest. I mean you have to know how to zig when your competitor expects you to zag. You have to have an unquenchable appetite for success—the entrepreneur is always reaching for new challenges.

"You also have to have a good mate. In the early days, when things looked bleak and I would come home beat, Lois always encouraged me to keep trying. To this day, she says, 'So what if we end up with a hamburger stand?' When you have that kind of a wife, you can't miss." Yet Jeno believes in keeping home and work separate. "I don't hang around the house during the day, and she doesn't come to the office," he says. Lois Paulucci has her own busy life, rich with family and community activities. Either have a mate like that, Jeno says, or stay single.

He has similar advice regarding partnerships. "You have to have a feeling of fierce independence, knowing that often times you are alone," he says. "When I had a partner, I was spending more time wondering whether *he* was going to do the job or whether *I* was going to do the job, and sometimes neither one of us did the job. I decided it was better to know I had to do it myself. Besides, I have a partner: the U.S. government takes half the profits—why have somebody else take half of what's left? If you're small and want to grow, you shouldn't have any partners if you can help it, because after the government takes its 50 percent you still need money for capital growth."

The most difficult aspect of his business, Jeno says, has been learning to delegate. "As your organization grows, you have to be able to delegate—and hire the best people possible. You can't do it on your own. As long as you communicate and control, you'll know when a person is working or not working out."

But the presidency of Jeno's, Inc., has been something of a revolving door since Paulucci stepped down. Restraining that "gale-force" personality has not been easy. "The only time I ever feel depressed is when I'm dealing with persons I know are doing something totally wrong, and yet because I don't want to kill their spirit I have to go easy and use psychology. I don't want to destroy them or create enemies. It just becomes one hell of a problem. In the end, I won't let anybody or anything stand in my way."

He says he still smarts from childhood humiliations: "Being called a dirty wop, a dago, and Wasp children not being allowed to play with me." Yet growing up poor, the son of an immigrant on the "wrong side of the tracks," had its positive side, too: "It gave me a fire in my spirit, a desire to prove I was as good as anyone in this country—not *better* than anyone else, but as good. It made me adopt a spit-in-the-eye philosophy and a desire to be a success."

His greatest obstacle, he says, was "the cynics in the Duluth business community who wondered what that dago from the Iron Range—that fruit-stand barker—was doing coming in here to grow bean sprouts." But even when the banks turned him down, Jeno seldom thought about giving up. "The idea of having to work for someone else rather than being my own boss was enough to make me spit in the eyes of those bankers and find somebody else who would give me the capital."

His "typical" day is a fugue of details as he attends to the business, civic and philanthropic projects in which he's continually involved. He chairs, for example, the National Italian American Foundation, and, in 1979, he ventured into publishing with *Attenzione*, an elegant magazine he recently sold to a New York publishing firm. Ever a maverick, Jeno has been active in numerous election campaigns. He supported Hubert Humphrey in 1968, then served as vice chairman of a committee of prominent independents supporting Richard Nixon in 1972. Working for John Connally in that campaign gave him a bleeding ulcer, he says—but he cured himself with bananas, Gelusil and will power.

His political efforts have not, however, been limited to presidential elections. He founded and still chairs the

Northeastern Minnesota Organization for Economic Education (NEMO, Inc.), the organization that lobbied for the Minnesota Taconite Amendment, the act that enabled northeastern Minnesota to attract and support taconite mining and processing through the 1960s. At the first NEMO meeting, Paulucci earned an "undying reputation for bad taste" by setting up gravestones on the grounds of the meeting hall, each gravestone representing some company or industry that once flourished in the area but had since died. In 1970, he financed a Stanford Research Institute study that became the grounds for a proposed taconite production tax (that would keep some earnings from mining in the state). The tax was tied to the price of steel by the 1977 legislature, and Jeno proudly refers to that legislation as the "Paulucci Bill."

More recently, Jeno took on the sponsors of the so-called "Hostage Shop Bill" proposed in the 1981 legislature. "I don't believe in government *or* unions telling you when to close a plant, open a plant or reduce labor," he growls. "I told Skip Humphrey [one of the bill's sponsors] that his father would turn over in his grave. Liberal as he was, Hubert Humphrey was a realist, and he knew you just can't do things that ruin incentive for business to come in or stay in the state." And when Governor Al Quie announced plans to add a five percent surtax to the state income tax, Jeno reminded Quie of his campaign stance against higher taxes and accused him of talking out of both sides of his mouth.

Paulucci has even taken on the U.S. State Department. He visited earthquake-devastated Italy twice, in 1976 and in 1980. "When I went there for President Ford," he says, "I saw right away that what they needed was expertise in engineering and architecture that was not available in small towns. I thought, what an opportunity for business to get involved, especially the multinationals who are very suspect in Italy. I called a meeting in Milan, and we had a luncheon with the American Chamber of Commerce. I got up and told them what I had seen and what was needed. 'You folks have a great opportunity to lend technical people for three or six months to help rebuild these towns,' I said. 'Not only will you be doing good, but all of Italy and all of Europe will know about it.' I told them what we do in Minnesota—I told them about Dayton Hudson and the

Five Percent Club.

"They looked at me like I was a Communist. They couldn't get me out of there fast enough. The next day I called a press conference, and the State Department damn near had me shot. They tried to take my press release and rewrite it, but every time I would just write a new one."

Back home, Jeno built on the Five Percent Club idea, proposing a "President's Council on Business Responsibility" composed of regional councils and business-responsibility groups working with the government. He presented the plan to President Ford ("He liked it") and, after the 1976 election, to President Carter ("It was like talking to a wall. He didn't understand it"). President Reagan has the plan now, and Jeno's friend Walter Mondale is also studying it.

When formal proposals and lobbying efforts don't work, Jeno often turns to the media or even prints his own materials. Some are full-page, open letters to the people of Minnesota ("I am asking business leaders and politicians to put up or shut up with their derogatory remarks and unfounded charges that the Minnesota business climate is not good") or President Reagan ("Forget your Kemp-Roth tax cut campaign promise"). Others are aggressive little pamphlets with titles such as, "Wake Up: We're 100 Years Too Late," "If You Don't Enjoy Rape, Holler" and "Proof that Small Business Is Becoming an Endangered Species." None of this comes as a surprise to the people of Minnesota. In 1961, Jeno bought a half-hour of television time to chide the legislature for debating about a state bird while ignoring the taconite bill. He made his point by talking to a loon.

☐ Some of Paulucci's projects have died, but not for lack of effort. He campaigned long and hard for a "Missing Link Waterway," a canal that would have joined the Mississippi River with the Great Lakes. He's crusaded for the development of Harbor Mall in downtown Duluth and worked hard to secure commitments from major department stores to locate there, so far to no avail.

Some of Paulucci's business ventures have failed as well. Others have just not been completely successful—which, for Jeno, is the same thing. Wilderness Valley Farms (7,000 acres of farmland growing celery in northern Minnesota) might have worked, if Jeno had somehow been able to lengthen the growing season. A water chestnut-growing operation in Florida was another loser. The water chestnuts grew beautifully, but the cost of labor to peel them was prohibitive. Raising wild rice in Minnesota was still another loser, as was the First Sierra Corporation, a mutual fund Jeno bought after he sold Chun King. An irradiation process for preserving food was yet another.

The Cornelius Company, a Minneapolis-based manufacturer of beverage and food-service equipment, has proved a headache since Paulucci invested $2 million. After watching operations founder, he became chairman of the board and set about straightening out the company. Then, in 1981, four Cornelius stockholders filed a class-action suit claiming the Paulucci family, in owning more than 50 percent of the stock, depressed the price and restricted trading activity. But late in the year, Cornelius had an acquisition offer from a Birmingham, England, firm at a price few stockholders could refuse.

Then there are the restaurants. Jeno Paulucci has tried and failed seven times. Those strike-outs are particularly distressing to Jeno's competitive spirit because his son Mick hit a home run with his first, Grandma's, an old refurbished bar right across the street from Jeno's, Inc. When Mick approached his dad with the idea, Jeno recalls, "I told him to make a parking lot."

Business for Jeno is always business. When the cost of transporting frozen pizza from Duluth to Eastern and Southern markets became prohibitive, Paulucci announced that the company was forced to move its Duluth manufacturing operations (though not its headquarters) to a more centrally located Ohio site. The switch means the loss of nearly 1,300 jobs for Duluth, and it was an especially sensitive issue for Paulucci, a former "Employer of the Year" and untiring champion of northeastern Minnesota.

Jeno's, Inc., and Jeno himself were besieged with letters and reporters' calls. Each writer received a reply and a thorough explanation of the economic reality that forced the move. The more vitriolic letters, however, were returned with Jeno's famous "screw you" stamp. And Jeno began looking for other companies to replace the jobs lost by his company's action.

Like most successful people, Paulucci receives an enormous number of requests for charitable contributions. Formal donations are made through the Paulucci Family Foundation. Informal gifts are sometimes spontaneous, and they often leave the recipients thinking lightning has struck.

Paulucci's friend Frank Befera, a prominent Duluth businessman who grew up with him in Hibbing, recalls an Arctic fishing trip a few years back. He and Jeno had learned of an isolated Indian village whose annual food shipment was delayed by late-breaking ice. Jeno decided to come to the rescue. He and Befera flew to the nearest town, 250 miles away, and headed for the only grocery store, only to find it closed. Undaunted, they called a cab and located the two owners, awakened them and persuaded them to return to the store. Shopping list in hand, Jeno put together the biggest sale the grocers had ever seen. Another cab was called, and 2,000 pounds of food was put aboard while Paulucci and the grocers prepared to settle up.

"What's my discount?" Paulucci asked.

"No discount," said one of the grocers.

"I've been in business all my life," said Jeno, "and I *always* get a discount. Twenty percent."

"No discount."

To Befera's amazement, Jeno ordered the cab driver to unload the 2,000 pounds of food. No discount, no sale.

"They settled on a 15 percent discount," Befera remembers. "Jeno tipped the drivers $50 each. When he strikes a bargain, he'll try to whittle off the bottom line. But when it comes to giving something away, he's very generous."

Although he insists he is still, in many ways, the little Hibbing kid with the red wagon, there are signs that Jeno sometimes stops to contemplate what he has accomplished. He is proud of his son Mick's growing skill and early successes. And he reflects on his own. "I don't think the bottom line is whether you have made a million or a billion, but what you have done with your life," he says. "How you have raised your family, what you have done within your state, community and nation. And what you have done with your heritage."

As for retirement—well, says Jeno, "I wouldn't think of it. I'll retire when they pat me on the face with the shovel."

Earl Bakken

2

Earl Bakken

Sparks of Life

His basement workshop in a tidy, blue-collar neighborhood of northeast Minneapolis was quite possibly unique. Everywhere you looked there were dusty vacuum tubes, stray circuits, copper wire, electrician's tape, Erector Set parts and scrap wood. Dog-eared copies of *Popular Mechanics* were piled in a corner. A bomb was cooking on a hotplate.

Some kids in the neighborhood considered the basement workshop Earl Bakken's chamber of horrors. But to the nine-year-old Bakken, it was the sanctuary where he built his "shock machine" and countless radios, the retreat where he designed a lighted scoreboard for a high school athletic field and constructed a private telephone hooked up to a friend's home and complete with amplifier earphones borrowed from a gracious, near-deaf grandmother.

It was also the place where the youthful Bakken built his robot. A five-foot-tall robot whose skeleton was Erector Set pieces and "flesh" was plywood. A robot with blinking red eyes and a head that moved up and down, smoking a

Lucky Strike. The robot was a chain smoker, in fact, thanks to the ingenious connection Bakken made between a hot-water bottle that served as the robot's lungs and an electric motor seated in the robot's ample mid-section.

The robot was inevitable. Bakken spent his Saturday afternoons soaking up the minute details of every Frankenstein movie that came to town. The idea of using electricity to bring a creature to life fascinated him. And while his own creature was not the equal of that Celluloid anti-hero, the idea took hold. Electricity and life. One impulse sparking another.

Bakken's experimentation knew few limits in those days. He was an only child for the first 18 years of his life, and his doting parents fed his curiosity. Florence Bakken scoured the basement at Dillman's hardware store for stray vacuum tubes, wires and switches. She lobbied the local radio repairman for first pick of his cast-off parts. An avid reader, Osval Bakken kept his son well-stocked with *Popular Mechanics* as well as with workshop tools.

The boy was given to solitude and experimentation. He had only a few close friends. Joe Colianni, who lived at the other end of that makeshift telephone Bakken created, was one friend; Harry Zook, with whom Bakken had a "pact," was another. Bakken and Zook cloistered themselves in the Bakken basement most evenings and weekends. They needed little else in their youth but this.

"That kid is going to electrocute himself some day," Osval Bakken's brother shouted, spotting Earl absorbed in yet another experiment. This time the boy was in the Bakken attic, alone.

It had been a quiet day until the explosion. There was a sudden flash of light.

"For God's sake, Earl—what now?" Osval shouted.

The boy was exploding firecrackers, but not in the conventional manner. Rather than light them with common matches, Earl was setting off each fuse with a live electrical wire. Snap, sizzle, out the window—*boom!*

It was enough to turn Florence Bakken's hair prematurely gray. But Florence was a willing accomplice of her son. She poked around for spare parts, she lent him her spare hotplate so he could stir up a chemical bomb in the basement. She even submitted herself to Earl's scary "shock machine." Florence shakes her head today. "But what if we had stopped him?'' she asks. It's a fair enough question.

If the Bakkens *had* stopped their mad-scientist son tinkering with electricity in the basement, there might not be a Medtronic, Inc., selling more than 90,000 implantable pacemakers annually for heart patients around the world. Earl Bakken and his brother-in-law, Palmer Hermundslie, founded the company in 1949. Today, Medtronic is a more than $300-million-a-year enterprise manufacturing pacemakers in such far-flung locations as Canada, Puerto Rico, the Netherlands, France and Brazil, and selling them in 75 countries worldwide.

Medtronic's psychic center is still just a few miles away from the Bakkens' Northeast basement. Medtronic has always been close to Earl Bakken's boyhood home. In many respects, those early years were the best in Earl Bakken's life. Solitary, experimental, uncomplicated—quite different from the years that followed, years that turned Bakken from an engineer into a reluctant entrepreneur. Indeed, the events in the life of Medtronic seemed to shape Earl Bakken more than he shaped them.

□ The Bakken family kept to themselves. Osval, a full-blooded Norwegian, worked as an office clerk at a nearby manufacturing company. He spent his evenings reading fiction, working crossword puzzles or untangling math problems. Math was Osval's hobby—he inherited it from his father, and young Earl developed the same interest. When he wasn't working electric magic in the basement, Earl Bakken was poring over geometry problems from an old college textbook. Florence Bakken ran the household and served as secretary at the First Lutheran Church of Columbia Heights, three blocks from home. She, too, was a math ace.

Earl Bakken had time to bloom. He worked few childhood jobs and had a regular, albeit modest, allowance from his parents—enough to spend on hot-water bottle ''lungs'' to install in a robot. Bakken told his mother he ''didn't have time'' to go out for high school football, although he eventually won a letter in track.

Bakken was the kind of kid that haunts every high school—he carried a briefcase, and he always knew how to make the recalcitrant film projector work. He was serious and bright. Not a leader, but a very able practitioner. He was graduated with above-average grades, earned with a modicum of study. Rather than diagram a sentence or study the Spanish Civil War, he'd always preferred to design the ultimate robot.

Upon graduation from Columbia Heights High School in December 1941, Bakken headed for the University of Minnesota to earn an electrical engineering degree. Not long into his studies, however, he was ready to enlist, eager to be part of the "big war." He joined the Army Signal Corps, hoping to be assigned to radio work. Instead he was given a three-month radar course and sent to Florida for further training. He was later transferred to the Air Corps to fully utilize his radar skills.

He studied for a third-class radio-telephone license test, took it, and finished so quickly that the man in charge suggested he try the second-class test the same day. "While you're here," the man added, "why not fill out a first-class test, too." Bakken did. A few months later he received the results. He had passed all three tests in one day, which was enough to qualify him immediately as a radar instructor.

When the war was over, Bakken returned to the University of Minnesota and resumed his electrical engineering studies on the GI Bill. Surprisingly, for a young man whose high school grades had come so easily, classes were tough. And, when Bakken's brother-in-law, a lumberyard manager, traded small talk at a family birthday party in 1949, the idea of starting a company of his own appealed to him.

Bakken had married a medical technologist working at Northwestern Hospital, Connie Olson. Evenings, after studying at the university, he drove to Northwestern to wait until his wife finished her shift. To kill time, the consummate tinkerer fixed stray medical devices—an electrocardiograph that skipped too many beats, a centrifuge that stopped dead. Hospital engineers, in those days, were equipped only to fix heavy machinery like elevators. Delicate instruments in disrepair were farmed out to local radio repair shops. Bakken could save the hospital a service call. He was quick to isolate the problem and willing to work as long as Connie Bakken was on duty.

The work was there to be done, Bakken told Palmer Hermundslie. So why not establish a local repair service for hospitals? Why not contact all the equipment manufacturers and find out precisely how to repair their delicate instruments? Why not learn how to calibrate the instruments to make them perform at their best? Why not tap the market? A couple of months after they asked themselves those questions, Bakken, then 25, quit graduate school, and Hermundslie, 30, left the northeast Minneapolis lumberyard, and together they started their own business.

Bakken had no capital to bring to the new partnership. In fact, Hermundslie lent Bakken money to invest in the original venture. Hermundslie, Bakken remembers, "begged, borrowed or wrote second mortgages on anything he had to get the enterprise moving."

From the beginning, the affable Hermundslie contributed his personality, business sense and fund-raising ability to the partnership. Bakken, in turn, aimed his analytical mind at repairs and designs for custom medical devices. For Bakken, it was much like being back in his parents' basement workshop again. Only this time, it was a garage.

Bakken and Hermundslie operated rent-free out of a 600-square-foot space in northeast Minneapolis. Lumber from old refrigerated boxcars lined the garage walls, and salvaged steel bars fortified the windows (even then, the pair worried about protecting trade secrets). A pot-bellied stove provided heat on cold days, and the building was cooled when Bakken or Hermundslie sprayed cold water on the roof. The two young men worked at hand-built benches and desks.

Hermundslie owned the garage. He also rented attic living quarters to Earl and Connie Bakken for a pittance. The Bakkens relied on Connie's salary to cover their living expenses. It was a time to live simply and to summon every resource.

In one of its first months of operation, Medtronic (an amalgam of "medical" and "electronic") made just $8 on the repair of one centrifuge. Things could only get better, the partners agreed. The repair business turned out to be no gold mine, so Bakken and Hermundslie found a sideline—they became manufacturers' representatives for medical-device companies whose equipment they repaired. Luckily, a leading electrocardiograph company, Sanborn, handed Bakken and Hermundslie the Upper Midwest territory.

The young men in the garage, meanwhile, were busy

learning all they could about medical terminology, anatomy and physiology. "We each took a subject," Bakken recalls. "Each person was responsible for studying that subject and then teaching it. We had to increase our knowledge by teaching ourselves."

Medtronic's sales work, while it was difficult for the introverted Bakken, put the partners in touch with local physicians and surgeons who asked them to design adaptors so the equipment they sold would work with existing systems. Bakken called the adaptors "specials," and he got a kick out of yet another chance to tinker. "We built two of this, five of that, eight of another," he says. "We made the specials mainly to help sell Sanborn equipment." Before long, Bakken was designing additional custom medical devices. "We tried to do everything," he explains. "We responded to every doctor who came along with a good idea. It seemed like a way to earn a buck, but we vastly underestimated our costs."

The partners were soon making everything—insulated forceps, blood gas shakers, defibrillators, animal respirators, cardiac rate monitors, a sophisticated little device designed to measure the size of animal cells under a microscope and add up those minute dimensions electronically. The product designs were simple sketches, and the parts were handmade or found in local surplus stores or radiotelevision shops. Medtronic now had a small production staff, which was led by Bakken and shared soldering irons and other tools. Each final product was wrapped in newspaper and delivered to customers in packing boxes local merchants had discarded. What did it matter if a Medtronic defibrillator arrived in an Oxydol carton? It was a custom-made special.

Return on investment mattered a great deal more to the struggling company. "We went way over our estimate on some specials," Bakken recalls. "We just weren't very sophisticated about money. We took the cost of our materials and multiplied that by five. I think I read that somewhere—I was reading every chance I got, mainly to try to understand business practices. Those custom products never sold the way we hoped they might. We were naive, and each special put us further in debt." Fortunately, more than half of Medtronic's revenue in the early 1950s came from the sale of other manufacturers' products.

☐ The implantable, transistorized pacemaker, however, was one custom device that sold many more than 10 for Medtronic.

It was sheer luck that brought Earl Bakken into the world of Dr. C. Walton Lillehei, a pioneer in open-heart surgery at the University of Minnesota. Bakken was selling Sanborn monitoring equipment to University Hospital about the time Lillehei was searching for a way to help youngsters past the delicate post-operative period when their weak hearts often failed them. These children, called "blue babies," were infants with congenital heart trouble who actually appeared blue because their blood lacked sufficient oxygen.

Bakken stood by during some of Lillehei's infant surgery to make sure his Sanborn equipment worked properly. After surgery, the infants often suffered "heart block," their hearts barely beating. These infants could not handle the large, external pacemakers available in the 1950s. Those pacemakers produced electric shocks that were often too traumatic for young hearts. Not only that, the pacemakers were plugged into AC wall sockets. They could—and did—fail during power outages.

Lillehei and his colleagues developed a better pacemaker for children that sent a lower voltage through wires attached directly to the heart. But power was still a concern. Lillehei had been through outages and seen AC-powered pacers fail. A thunderstorm one summer evening in 1957 shut off the university's electricity for six hours. Although the hospital had a back-up generator for its surgery and recovery rooms, patient rooms had no auxiliary power. The weakened hearts of some of Lillehei's patients slowed to only 20 or 30 beats per minute.

That did it. "Isn't there some way," Lillehei asked Bakken, "that we can power a pacemaker with a battery?"

Bakken pondered the question in the Medtronic garage. The electric pulse needed for a pacemaker was so small, it seemed to warrant a transistor. But how to make one? Bakken consulted a boyhood resource, *Popular Electronics,* and stumbled across a metronome circuit design. The circuit produced a rhythmic pulse that could speed up or slow down, depending upon the tune a pianist played. A rhythmic pulse. A heartbeat. Electricity and life. Bakken set to work in the garage.

"I took the circuit, modified it and got the right voltages for the heart," Bakken recalls. "I left the loudspeaker off from the metronome design, put on a couple terminals, and that was it. The entire process took only a few weeks."

Almost without missing a heartbeat, the university tested the new pacemaker on laboratory animals. Soon Lillehei strapped the first battery-operated Medtronic pacemaker—a device about the size of three cigarette packs carried in a canvas holder—to a small child's chest. It was an unqualified success.

Bakken and Hermundslie began to see that this custom device had promise well beyond five or 10 replicated models. But the real promise for Medtronic surfaced with two inventors in New York.

About the time Bakken was experimenting with a battery-powered pacemaker for Lillehei, Wilson Greatbatch, an electrical engineer based in upstate New York, was well on his way to designing a battery-operated, plastic-coated pacemaker that could be implanted in the human body. Greatbatch's lab was a barn loft behind his remodeled farmhouse. He worked alone on his project for two years because he had trouble interesting any doctor in his design. Then Greatbatch met Dr. William Chardack, chief of surgical services at the Veterans Administration Hospital in Buffalo. The pair teamed up.

Greatbatch and Chardack knew much about Medtronic and its work with Lillehei. They also knew about a "bipolar" electrode invented by Dr. Samuel Hunter of St. Joseph's Hospital in St. Paul and Norman Roth, one of Bakken's electrical engineers. That electrode could be attached to a defective heart and concentrate the electrical impulse where it was most needed. The Hunter-Roth electrode thus spared the patient excess electrical impulses that might eventually numb the heart. Greatbatch and Chardack put in a call to Medtronic. They wanted to incorporate that bipolar electrode into their implantable pacemaker design. Their call signaled the start of a 10-year collaboration.

On April 18, 1960, Dr. Chardack and his associate, Dr. Andrew Gage, attached a bipolar electrode to the heart of a 77-year-old retired optical-company inspector. For several weeks, the man's heart relied on an external pacemaker for the necessary electrical impulses. But less than two months later, after the man's condition had stabilized, Chardack and Gage turned his heart over to an implanted pacemaker designed by Wilson Greatbatch.

It was a medical milestone—the first successful implant, in a human body, of a self-contained pacemaker with its own power supply.

Bakken and Hermundslie didn't wait long to capitalize on that milestone. Hermundslie, the better salesman of the two partners and a pilot from World War II, flew to Buffalo in October 1960 to sign a contract with Greatbatch and Chardack giving Medtronic the exclusive right to produce and market their implantable pacemaker. A month later, production began in the Twin Cities, and by the end of December, Medtronic had 50 orders at $375 apiece. There were more orders for a single medical device than Bakken and Hermundslie had seen in 11 years.

The contract gave Chardack and Greatbatch tight control over Medtronic pacemaker manufacturing for a decade after that. They approved every drawing, every design change, every bit of communication to the medical community. "That tight licensing agreement meant we could affect the life of the company," Greatbatch says now. "It meant we could exert a stranglehold on Medtronic, had we wanted to. Medtronic's banker complained about it, but the arrangement continued that way for 10 years. It takes a special kind of sensitivity to own a company and give others a lot of rope. Earl Bakken could see the value of that."

Bakken also knew how mutually beneficial the arrangement was. He had demonstrated a knack for moving close to the "sources"—people like Lillehei, Hunter, Chardack and Greatbatch. He knew those people would be important to the future of Medtronic, and he diligently found ways to mobilize their abilities.

Most observers would have thought that 1960 and 1961 were banner years for the young pacemaker company, now operating out of a new 15,000-square-foot building in northeast Minneapolis. The Medtronic staff had grown from two partners to 54 people. The company had begun marketing its devices outside the United States through Picker International, a technical sales company, and Medtronic had 14 sales people of its own working the United States and Canada. Bakken and Hermundslie, moreover,

had expanded their line to include Telecor, a heart-
monitoring device; Cardiac Sentinal, an alarm system
designed to summon help and stimulate a failing heart with
electrical impulses; the Conduction System Locator, a
device that helps surgeons perform delicate heart operations; and a Coagulation Generator designed to control
bleeding during surgery. But while the product line was impressive, it was costly as well.

"Medtronic was still very small," Thomas Holloran,
once legal counsel and later Medtronic president, says.
"Medtronic had limited capital to withstand the down-
turns. At the same time, there was an explosion of knowledge in medical electronics. Earl and Palmer tried to move
too fast into too many markets, especially into heart monitoring, a particularly demanding area." Construction of
those monitors was expensive. In addition, substantial capital was tied up while the monitors were tested and "de-
bugged" at hospitals. The new devices were not an easy
sell. They required new techniques and new training that
some doctors did not willingly embrace. "During that era,
Medtronic had a bigger appetite for products than its capital could sustain," says Holloran.

The partners could have been criticized for misplaced
priorities. Where was their concern for quarterly profits?
Who was minding the bottom line? For Earl Bakken, the
definition of return on investment seemed to relate more to
research gains than to profit. That perspective was part of
his personal history. Making things that worked had more
appeal to the man than making money.

Tom Holloran says, "Bakken's first concern has never
been, What are our sales and profits this quarter? His first
concern has always been, What have we done to improve
the lives of human beings? Bakken was in business to deliver life-giving products to people. He was not in business
with an eye trained primarily on profit."

Manuel Villafana, Bakken's former employee and later
founder of arch-competitor Cardiac Pacemakers, Inc., offers a similar observation. "Once, when we listed the 10
primary objectives of Medtronic in a planning session,"
Villafana says, "profit wasn't even on the list."

But profit became the primary issue in 1961. Medtronic
had to have it if it wanted to survive.

"We added more people than the rate of sales growth

justified," Bakken recalls. "So by 1960, we were, for all practical purposes, bankrupt. Palmer was doing the money-raising, and he was good at that. I was doing technical development, engineering and sales. But between us, there was no real long-range planning, no real control of our growth. Medtronic was doing things all over the map," he says, pointing to a grid with 16 squares—filled with the names of medical devices ranging from breath simulators to potency detectors. "We were producing in almost all the squares—devices for x-ray departments, devices for animal husbandry. But we couldn't afford to make and market them all."

Medtronic had splintered its attention and capital among too many products. Furthermore, the Medtronic sales force seemed to prefer selling only pacemakers— that's where the commissions were. Although sales grew from $180,000 to more than $500,000 from 1960 to 1962, the company suffered severe losses. There was not enough capital for Medtronic's expanding sales network, for its ambitious new-product research, for expensive front-end manufacturing, for generous travel budgets aimed at sending many Medtronic employees to teaching seminars and medical conventions. (Medtronic had been dubbed the "U of M," largely because Bakken was so committed to teaching employees about the human body. Production staffers took anatomy classes. Salesmen knew the medical lingo cold. They also took speech courses to improve their delivery. Secretaries learned the function of a myocardial lead. Bakken's long-standing commitment to education was expensive.)

Those were grim days in the early 1960s. Northwestern National Bank would have been justified in calling in its $150,000 loan. In the meantime, Palmer Hermundslie's health was beginning to deteriorate because of chronic diabetes; he was also going blind. Earl Bakken, the engineer, was left in charge of the near-terminal company. Bakken had said some years earlier that without Hermundslie's tenacity and belief in the business, the partnership would not have lasted. Now Bakken had to summon his own tenacity.

"That was a crucial turning point for me," Bakken says. "My pleasure had always been in making devices. Building them, delivering them, seeing them work. In my youth, I never planned to become head of a major manufacturing company. My goal was to be just a research engineer, doing my thing in some corner of some company like Honeywell. I'd always been extremely introverted, so management and doing things that managers do was not my goal. I had no other plans but to hide someplace.

"Medtronic's board of directors took me aside and said, 'You have to decide. Are you going to continue creating medical devices or will you be president of Medtronic?' That decision weighed heavily on me. But I made the decision to try management and to manage through people rather than manage directly. I didn't know a lot about business, but I read a lot—everything I could get my hands on. With the help of our board, I believed I would make the transition from engineer to businessman. If I hadn't made that decision, I believe Medtronic would have folded. It looked like no one else was willing to step in."

Only one company demonstrated an interest in acquiring the flagging Medtronic at a bargain price in 1961. That was P.R. Mallory, manufacturer of the mercury-zinc battery used in Medtronic pacemakers. Mallory's management explored the idea of acquisition, but finally decided that the pacemaker market was not very promising. Mallory never made a firm offer. If it had, Bakken says now, "we would have sold."

Left without an offer or an active partner, Bakken dug in. "I had to fire half our people. We went from 54 employees down to 27. We began doing a lot of planning, developing yearly budgets, setting clear objectives. We cut out a good share of our product line and concentrated on implantable pacemakers. We had some fantastic instruments, but we had to cut them out of our minds."

Bakken set down Medtronic's objectives, and those objectives have guided the company ever since. Medtronic would: contribute to human welfare; direct its growth in biomedical engineering; gather skilled people; build the staff with education; strive for the greatest possible reliability and quality in its products. "To make a fair profit" came fourth on the corporate list.

☐ In early 1962, Northwestern National Bank of Minneapolis came through with $100,000 in long-term financing for Medtronic. Community Investment Enterprises,

Inc., a young venture-capital firm based in Minneapolis, bought approximately one-third of Medtronic with the purchase of $200,000 in convertible debentures. CIE's William Dietrich and Gerald Simonson joined the Medtronic board of directors. One or the other visited almost daily to monitor the company's accounts payable and receivable.

Fiscal 1962-63 sales crested at $985,000, with profits of $73,000 for the year. By fiscal 1963-64, Medtronic's sales reached $1.59 million, with earnings of $151,000. The steady growth curve was leading Medtronic to an extraordinary year. Sales for the year ended April 30, 1968, totaled $9.95 million, up 98 percent over total sales for the year before. Earnings ballooned by 128 percent over 1967, and Medtronic's shares outstanding grew by six percent. Fiscal 1968-69 was even better. Sales increased to $15.3 million, up 54 percent, and earnings rose 19 percent over the previous year.

"Medtronic is in an emerging field—medical electronics," one analyst said at the time. "The company has a shot at being a leader in the industry. People who are buying Medtronic stock are professionals—institutions and large individual investors—looking at three to five years from now; people who know the risk. They're taking a shot at a super growth company."

Worldwide, Medtronic had captured more than 50 percent of the pacemaker market by 1968.

For his part, Earl Bakken was learning to behave—and to look—presidential. "In the early years, Earl was the lumberjack-shirted engineer with a soldering iron in one hand," Manny Villafana recalls. "Then, during the 1960s, he developed. It was like someone going to finishing school. He became an excellent speaker, he became educated in the finer things, he dressed better. He went about it all in his own quiet way. Wilhemine Saucier, Earl's executive secretary and later a vice president, had a hand in shaping him. When she joined Medtronic in 1965, Earl was an engineer. When she left, he was truly a CEO."

"Earl realized that a person's ability to succeed is limited by his ability to communicate," Saucier says. "We spent hours working on speeches Earl was to deliver. I became his audience and coach. Also, when I first went to work for Earl, he wore white socks and pants too short, and he was 40 pounds overweight. He said to me one day, 'Billie, I can't be a CEO, I'm an engineer.' "

That changed. Bakken began dressing in three-piece suits from Young-Quinlan. He took up ballroom dancing as a hobby, and he began traveling. Overcoming his fear of air travel, he took sales trips to Belgium, the Netherlands, Germany, and later to Russia, Hong Kong and the People's Republic of China. "The object," Saucier says, "was to get him out of suburban Minneapolis."

Bakken knew, too, that it was important to staff the executive offices with others who could communicate effectively. He invited Tom Holloran, then an attorney with Wheeler and Fredrikson, to sign on as Medtronic's president. Holloran, in fact, was to be a second Palmer Hermundslie—the public personage to Bakken's emerging CEO. Holloran was asked to stand in the forefront, while Bakken coached quietly from within. (Later, that "upfront" role was assumed by Dale Olseth, formerly director of research for Dain, Kalman & Quail and still later president of Tonka Corporation.)

When Wilson Greatbatch and Medtronic severed their association over a performance disagreement, Bakken began bolstering his research-and-development capabilities. He hired Arthur Schwalm, an ace design engineer, and Whitney McFarlin, a physicist and nuclear engineer who had logged at least a decade in medical and scientific instrumentation before joining Medtronic.

By the 1970s, Medtronic was enjoying a confident 65 percent share of the market with its mercury-zinc-powered pacemakers. In 1972, however, four former Medtronic employees—Manny Villafana, Anthony Adducci, Arthur Schwalm and James Baustert—formed Cardiac Pacemakers, Inc., to produce long-lasting pacemakers powered by a new lithium battery. CPI acquired 10 percent of the market within just a few years. Then, in 1976, while working hard and fast to bring out its own lithium-powered unit, Bakken and Medtronic again found themselves in real trouble.

"Like McDonnell Douglas, manufacturer of the DC-10," says Dale Olseth, "we had cracks in our pylons."

The product was the Xytron, a mercury-zinc-powered pacemaker implanted in a patient. The Xytron suddenly stopped functioning.

"When a pacemaker konks out," Olseth says, "we know it in a hurry because the physician will immediately call. Minute amounts of body fluids found their way into some of our Xytron units. After a period of time, they shorted out. Statistically, it was a small sample, but we didn't know which pacemakers might leak. And there were thousands of them out there. So we had to go to all our customers, every doctor and every patient, and tell them they might have a device that might not work properly.

"We went through a period of real trauma. A lot of people—employees and customers—had enormous confidence and trust in this company and what it stood for. A number of them went through grief; they thought it was impossible for us to have a problem."

Earl Bakken was not the least of the grievers. He believed in Medtronic products, some say to a fault. His critics say Bakken waited too long to announce the Xytron problem and order a recall. Others, like Tom Holloran, insist it takes time to see any sort of meaningful pattern in product-failure reports from divers points around the country. A dozen failures does not a trend make. Whatever the industry verdict, Bakken was noticeably shaken by the Xytron problem. And he suffered the feedback first-hand.

"Xytron was the first unit with integrated miniature circuits," he says. "We gave it a great deal of testing before going to the market, but we didn't test long enough to see the impact after two years of use. The Xytron failure was a great personal disappointment to me. We tested it in every way we knew how. One of my greatest concerns was to produce the most reliable product possible. I traveled extensively, talking to doctors, trying to be as candid as possible. I was told to leave a lot of times, kicked out of a doctor's office even before I could make a case for Medtronic. It hurt." More than profitability, Medtronic's standing in the medical community was crucial to Bakken.

The company's share of the U.S. pacemaker market tumbled to just under 40 percent in 1978. "But," says Olseth, "since the Xytron, we've had the Xyrel, Mirel and the Spectrax pacemakers, and all of those products have been technical beauties of high reliability. We've been earning our way back to credibility through reliability. The company has gotten better, tougher, more disciplined—

and humbler.''

Early in 1980, Medtronic introduced a new generation of pacemakers containing the latest in micro-electronic circuitry. The lead product was Spectrax SX, a programmable unit that could be adjusted after it was implanted with a hand-held computer. With that advance, Medtronic's U.S. market share climbed back to more than 40 percent by late 1980, and by year end 1981, Medtronic's sales totaled $313.6 million.

Medtronic had learned not to stand still while others—like Cardiac Pacemakers—delivered heady innovations. And Earl Bakken learned how to rebound from a failure he found difficult to accept.

□ During his more than 30 years in business, Earl Bakken has lived for Medtronic. He has worked relentlessly for countless hours and developed few outside interests. One of his few concessions to leisure was a ballroom he had built in his suburban home; there he and Connie waltzed together and taught the finer points of ballroom etiquette to friends. But the Bakkens' marriage of 30 years ended in 1978, the victim, some say, of a life narrowed to the medical electronics industry. Earl Bakken lives alone now, still about five miles from Medtronic corporate headquarters and five miles from his boyhood workshop.

A long-time colleague calls Bakken a ''passive success'' —not the ''classic'' entrepreneur fired with ambition or motivated by dreams of status and great wealth. All along, it would seem, Earl Bakken has been sparked by different rhythms.

Marvin Schwan

3

Marvin Schwan

The Emperor of Ice Cream

Anyone who thinks a successful business can be built in a year or two should drive on out to Marshall, Minnesota, and talk to Marvin Schwan.

It's not that Schwan has had many bad years. He hasn't really had any. But he has had his share of disasters, including fires and floods, and plenty of administrative puzzles as his privately held corporation grew from scratch to 4,000 employees in 48 states and $368 million a year in sales. In fact, it's taken more than 30 years of steady, careful step-by-step planning and hard work by this soft-spoken man from bustling headquarters in his farm-country hometown.

Marvin Schwan's success story really begins with his father. Born in Germany at the turn of the century, Paul Schwan left his homeland in the bitter, inflation-ridden years after World War I for a new life in America. He was welcomed into the community of hard-working German folk who had settled around Marshall, in southwestern Minnesota. After a few months as a railroad worker, he landed a job with the Marshall creamery, picking up milk and delivering ice cream to stores in a horse-drawn wagon. Paul found a bride, too, a bright, industrious farm girl named Alma Stelter. They were married in 1924, and within seven years they had a family of three boys, Alfred, Marvin and Robert.

For almost 20 years, Paul Schwan worked for others— first for the Marshall Creamery, then the Marshall Ice Cream Company—and dreamed of being his own boss. Finally, in 1941, he seized the chance: half interest in a milk-bottling plant adjacent to the Marshall Ice Cream Company. He and his partner named their firm Neisen and Schwan's Dairy. It was a family business built on hard work and long hours. Paul Schwan bottled milk from nearby dairy farms and delivered it at dawn to Marshall homes. The dairy and the ice cream factory provided after-school and summer jobs for the Schwan boys.

Marvin, Paul's second son, dreamed of earning enough money to go to college. At 14, he took on a 5:30 to 7 a.m. milk-delivery route. And on weekends—from early Saturday morning until late Saturday night and from 4 a.m. Sunday until 10:30 church—Marvin and his older brother Alfred packaged popsicles, fudgesicles and ice cream bars for the ice cream company. Summers, they packaged the ice cream novelties full-time.

The $12 Marvin made every week as a youthful milkman was steady, dependable income. But at the piece rate of three cents per dozen, his earnings at the ice cream factory depended on how fast, how long and how efficiently he could fill the envelopes with frozen treats.

When Alfred, at 18, enlisted in the Navy, Marvin was determined to carry on alone. He spied a trade-journal advertisement for a small machine that would blow bags open with air, and it set him thinking about efficiency. He sent for the machine with his own money—much to his employer's surprise. But Marvin guessed right. His efficiency increased 25 percent, and the boss paid him for the machine. Marvin could package 50 dozen fudgesicles in an hour to earn a respectable wage of $1.50. His education fund grew steadily.

Through the 1940s, the Schwan household was filled with energetic teenagers. The family dining room drew neighborhood boys for nightly homework sessions, with big dishes of ice cream or creamy malted milks passed around just before curfew. In that home, there was always room for one more boy, recalls Milford Paxton, then a young commercial artist who was taken into the family like a brother.

Marvin Schwan was intrigued with the paintings Paxton worked on during the evenings. Encouraged by an art teacher, Marvin turned out watercolors of his own. But painting was only one of his interests. He also loved to read, often waking early to pore over books on history or religion. From the ninth grade on, he lettered in football. And he studied hard, finally graduating at the top of his class in 1948. He is remembered to this day as a shy, sensitive boy whose intelligence drew the respect of his classmates. "Marvin was always way ahead of the rest of us," one old friend recalls.

☐ In a strong Lutheran community, the best and the brightest are often destined for the ministry, and Marvin Schwan seemed no exception. He enrolled at Bethany, a small, two-year college overlooking the Minnesota River Valley in Mankato, 100 miles from home. A college roommate and lifelong friend, Larry Bergdorf, now a pastor in St. Louis, remembers. Marvin Schwan, says Bergdorf, was a brilliant student—but a "lousy" speller. Also, Marvin was frugal, determined to live within a self-imposed budget of $15 a week. On weekends, Schwan returned to Marshall to package ice cream bars—often with the help of a time-and-motion study he'd puzzled over during the week. And after two years in college, Marvin knew he wanted just one thing: to try his hand at business.

It couldn't have been a better-timed decision. In 1948, Paul Schwan had bought out his partner and renamed the business Schwan's Dairy. Paul and Alma Schwan put everything they had into the enterprise. With help from Marvin, who invested his own savings as a partner, they built a new plant on South Second Street. The family moved into one of the six apartments on the second floor, and they hired five workers: two plant men, two route drivers and a part-time typist-clerk. The front of the building became Schwan's Dairy Store and a small restaurant where Alma Schwan fed customers hearty meals.

To make use of cream left over after milk was bottled in the dairy, Paul Schwan bought a counter-top ice cream maker. He perfected recipes for vanilla and chocolate ice cream and began turning out two-and-a-half-gallon batches at the rate of 10 gallons an hour. In 1950, when Marvin returned to this modest business, his job was to manage the dairy store.

In those early years, there was little left after Schwan's Dairy made its mortgage payments and met its payroll. "It was a real struggle," Marvin Schwan says. "We earned our wages, but that was all." Then, in 1951, a freeze on retail prices for milk nearly destroyed all the family had worked for. "The price to the farmers was not frozen," Schwan recalls. "During part of 1951, we paid more for the milk than we could sell it for. We were headed for bankruptcy."

At year's end, the dairy's credit rating was so low it could not buy its annual produce bond (a way of guaranteeing farmers they'd be paid for the milk they sold). In June 1952, the Schwans received a telegram from the State of Minnesota ordering them to cease operations immediately. It was a dark hour. As a last resort, Paul Schwan went to an elderly Marshall attorney, Charlie De Reu, who agreed to bankroll a cash bond. The dairy operations continued, but so did the price freeze.

Marvin Schwan had another problem. "I wanted to get married," he says, "but I knew I couldn't while I was a partner in a losing business. One day, I noticed that the price of ice cream in Montevideo [his future bride's hometown] was 14 cents higher than in Marshall. It was higher in other towns as well. I began to wonder how I could sell ice cream in those towns without investing in freezer cabinets and advertising. Then I thought of all the farmers who were buying home freezers. I knew all about home delivery —I had a milk route at 14—so I decided to deliver ice cream to all those new freezers."

Marvin found a panel truck with cracks in the floor, loose doors and no heater—but the truck was available at a price he could manage: $100. One early spring morning, he packed 17 gallons of his dad's chocolate and vanilla ice cream in dry ice and set out on his first route. By nightfall, he had sold all 17 gallons, and he knew his idea was worth keeping. Marvin turned the dairy store over to another employee and began cultivating customers with home delivery of the best ice cream in southern Minnesota.

After their wedding in September 1952, Marvin and

Mavis Schwan rose every day at 3 a.m., packed ice cream into containers and put the containers into the ancient panel truck. At 7 a.m., Marvin Schwan left Marshall with 25 gallons of vanilla, chocolate, strawberry and nine other flavors of ice cream. At 8 p.m. he returned home, almost always with an empty truck and a tidy profit.

Schwan became adept at freeing his truck from snowbanks and muddy, rutted country lanes. And he learned to face the ever-present farm dog: "I can match dog bite for dog bite with any one of you," he would tell his route drivers years later. In winter, he wiggled his toes to keep them from freezing and kept on selling, creating good will and making friends of farm families eager for the fresh ice cream packaged just that morning and brought to them by this polite and persistent young salesman. Marvin Schwan had found his business.

□ By the following spring, Schwan had more customers than he could serve alone. His truck was packed to capacity every day with 120 gallons of ice cream. He bought another truck and asked his friend Milford Paxton to paint it a creamy yellow and to create a logo. With a second driver, Schwan could sell almost 300 gallons of ice cream a day in one-gallon cartons and the distinctive, returnable two-and-a-half-gallon round cans that became his trademark.

With each week, Schwan ventured farther and farther from Marshall. No matter where he went, he found customers who had heard about his ice cream and were eager to buy. He began figuring how large a truck he'd need to stay on the road for two, even three days. In June 1953, when he learned of a half-ton panel truck he could buy for $1,000, he hired another driver.

But the overhead and the cost of building new routes began eating into his profit. "That second year, the three of us cleared only as much as I had made alone," he says. Undaunted, he knew that volume was the answer. And by 1954, Schwan's operation was big enough to hold an honest-to-goodness sales meeting: There were six routemen driving a fleet of five trucks—three refrigerated, two packed with insulated bags and ice.

By 1955, a salesman-driver named Butch Holtz was taking his Studebaker truck as far as the rolling farm country around Montgomery, more than 100 miles away. Schwan's ice cream became so popular with Montgomery farmers that Holtz couldn't fill all his orders with a single trip. "So I bought a 32-foot, single-axle semi-trailer, loaded it full of ice cream and hauled it to Montgomery," Schwan says. "It was our first depot." The depot concept worked out so well that Butch Holtz moved to Montgomery in 1956 and stored several days' worth of ice cream for his route in the trailer. It was another idea worth keeping.

Then Schwan weighed the cost of building depots and transporting ice cream to them against the alternative— growth restricted by geographic limits—and constructed his first 16-by-24-foot freezer-warehouse, in Sauk Centre. It was a crucial and profitable move: The added sales increased plant volume and lowered production costs.

Marvin Schwan began to see prospective sales well beyond Minnesota's borders. His modest company, just five years old, was on solid footing and ready to grow. But, in 1957, melting snow and spring rains pushed the Redwood River over its banks. For four days, Schwan's employees watched helplessly as muddy water covered their equipment and supplies. When the water subsided, employees worked hand in hand with the Schwan family to clean the plant and resume production. A federal disaster loan was repaid in a year because the terms of the loan made growth difficult, and grow was what Schwan intended to do.

Every year, the pace at Schwan's accelerated. In 1961, three new bookkeepers, an office manager, four plant workers and 16 new route drivers were added—along with 10 loaders, 22 trucks, two trailers, three depots and a number of new products. "If these farm families appreciate having ice cream delivered to their doors," Schwan reasoned, "why not bring them other products as well?" He began adding milk strainers, frozen fish and other items appreciated by customers located far from retail stores.

Marshall citizens watched in amazement as the Schwan plant expanded. A new garage was soon converted to a cooler, then to a deep freeze, and then the process would begin again. Sales figures kept pace: By 1962, sales for the dairy and the ice cream company totaled $4.5 million.

Then, on a hot July evening, a roaring fire destroyed an adjacent auto dealership. Again, Schwan's employees came to help rescue their company. They reinforced the ice cream plant's north wall to keep a 10-ton condenser from crashing through to the first floor. Within a year, the site of the auto dealership was added to Schwan's expanding headquarters. In the summer of 1963, two 12-hour shifts churned out more than 11,000 gallons of ice cream a day.

☐ That year was a milestone in other ways, too. It had been 15 years since Paul Schwan had struck out alone. While he had started with five employees, the company that Marvin now managed employed 117, with a payroll of more than $500,000. If the company was going to grow further, Marvin Schwan decided, it would have to be by acquisition. He began a program of careful purchases, buying companies with food products that could be distributed by his direct-to-the-customer method. A condensed-fruit juice company and a prepared sandwich company were added, and Schwan incorporated the acquisitions under a holding company he named Schwan's Sales Enterprises.

By 1965, pizza had overtaken the all-American burger in the appetites of farmers and city dwellers alike. A Schwan's salesman in Wisconsin began buying Roma-brand frozen pizzas and carrying them on his route. Schwan negotiated a contract to sell the pizzas in four states, and, by 1969, the flat pies were almost as popular as his ice cream. Pizza, Schwan figured, was here to stay. But when he asked Roma to expand sales beyond the four states, he was rebuffed.

"So I asked our comptroller to put an ad in the *Wall Street Journal*: 'Wanted to Buy: Pizza Plant,' the ad said. Believe it or not, we got a response!" The plant, Tony's Pizza, in Salina, Kansas, was just about perfect. It was centrally located, it had an easy-to-remember name, it was well-designed and modern. It had only one problem: the pizza. Schwan instructed the plant manager and a salesman to come up with a new recipe as good as, if not better than, Roma's. Schwan himself would be the final judge. Two days a week, Marvin Schwan and his brother Alfred (who now manages the plant) flew to Salina to test the results. Methodically, they tasted their way through vats of pizza sauce, beginning with basic tomato paste and adding spices one at a time. They tested crusts, then sausage and pepperoni. When Marvin decided the recipe was perfect, he began making pizza.

Schwan's insistence on top-quality products dictated a marketing system that didn't keep pizza sitting, flavor deteriorating, in chain-store warehouses. He decided to distribute the pizza the same way he did ice cream: direct from plant to customer. But this time, the customers were retail stores—including mom and pop operations—and the delivery vehicles were squarish, white two-ton trucks with Tony's logo in red and black.

It was a big step, and Schwan wasn't leaving anything to chance. Profits from each pizza route were computed at the end of each *day*, as well as at the end of each week and month. And profits there were. Schwan began adding new trucks to his fleet in rapid-fire succession.

There were also crises. Schwan was in New York at a sales meeting on Saturday, February 23, 1974, when he learned that a fire had started that afternoon in his Marshall ice cream plant. Hours later, he joined employees and townspeople to watch the blaze roar through the structure he had created. When the last embers died the next day, employees began sorting through the ashes for salvageable equipment. The telephone company set up an emergency phone system, and the office staff took up quarters in an old bank building. The payroll computer disk was flown to Fairmont, Minnesota, and printed there. Schwan found a Rochester company that would make the ice cream mix according to his father's recipe, and cold storage units were opened in Fort Dodge, Iowa. Town officials in Marshall met to say they were behind Schwan and would do everything they could to help him rebuild.

It was a time of soul-searching. The 1973 oil embargo had made transportation an increasingly costly expense. Schwan created computer models based on relocation to several other states. "It came down to a choice between staying in Marshall and moving to South Dakota," he says. "We looked at the cost of moving employees and training new people. The accounting firm's rule was our guide: Unless there is a five-percent advantage to moving, don't do it. We stayed. But Minnesota taxes have doubled since 1974, and I now think we should have moved." It was the most difficult decision of his career, he says.

☐ Today, Schwan's Sales Enterprises consists of 10 operating divisions. All but the original ice cream company are acquisitions, many of them suggested by Schwan employees in the field. Business Credit Leasing in Marshall and Syncom Magnetic Media, in Mitchell, South Dakota (manufacturer of computer tape, data-processing cassettes, diskettes, disk cartridges and disk packs), are the only nonfood divisions. For the other eight, transportation costs continue to be a major concern of Marvin Schwan. Since 1979, retail-route trucks have been converted to LP gas in an effort to reduce fuel costs. New trucks in the fleet of 1,000 are smaller and more fuel-efficient than their predecessors. At special "mapping meetings" drivers are encouraged to exchange stops and condense routes. Many drivers are adding overnight trips to their routes, just as Schwan had planned to do years earlier.

In the southwest Minnesota business community, Marvin Schwan is known as an innovative and aggressive businessman. John Suedbeck, president of Northwestern National Bank in Marshall, has known Schwan for 25 years. "I've always regarded him as a real brain, constantly dreaming up different ideas and promotions," Suedbeck says. "He has an ability to analyze, study and plan." As his organization grew, Suedbeck says, Schwan surrounded himself with loyal employees, many of them young locals whom he regarded as family. Schwan takes pride in his policy of promoting from within, although he recognizes the need for outside talent in special areas.

Schwan's attorney, Art Blaufuss, calls the entrepreneur a very unusual, complex man, a traditional person who believes in living up to his obligations and responsibilities. His community work is often indirect or undertaken as part of a team. "Marvin sits and thinks a lot," Blaufuss says. Much of his thinking these days is about the future of his business. The 1979 acquisition of Syncom Magnetic Media was notice that Schwan was, among other things, ready to diversify.

It's hard to imagine Schwan's Sales Enterprises headquartered anywhere but in Marshall. Although there now are Schwan plants in Kansas and South Dakota and sales divisions across the country, the company's heart remains in this rural Minnesota community. Schwan's is still a family business: Alfred Schwan oversees the ice cream plant, the sandwich plant and the Salina, Kansas, pizza plant; Robert Schwan is a company purchasing agent. Until 1978, when she retired at 77, Alma Schwan processed route bids in the bookkeeping department. (Paul Schwan died in 1969.) And even though Marvin lives across the border in Sioux Falls (site of the nearest commercial airport), he still belongs to Marshall.

A native son who succeeds on the scale achieved by Marvin Schwan might be faced with bitterness and jealousy. But Marshall residents are well aware of the jobs Schwan has created and the benefits his company brings to the community. Schwan's is known as a good place to work—an attitude reflected in the 120 to 200 applicants for the six to seven jobs that open up in an average month.

Schwan's treatment of employees could be characterized as enlightened paternalism. "I try to do what is fair from *their* point of view," he says. "In this organization, no one is considered better than anyone else. We have a structure in order to get things done. But the employees are all individuals, and I believe in treating them that way." That includes paying workers a wage that is fair for their geographic location, says long-time Schwan's employee Eddie Smith, plant manager and construction coordinator. "We expect a day's work for a day's wages, but we don't expect employees to work night and day. We know they have families and other interests."

Aggressively non-union, Schwan's has never had a layoff, Smith says. The company might close a department, but the employees are always given the opportunity to transfer to another. And Schwan's has provided work for people who traditionally might find jobs hard to come by —a convenience-food plant in Marshall's industrial park, for example, employs 100 workers, mainly young mothers whose schedules coincide with school hours. During the summer, these women can go on leave while college and high school students fill their jobs.

What's more, Marvin Schwan has always prided himself on knowing the names of all his employees. Now, when there are nearly 4,000 of them, it's an almost impossible task. Yet he attends 20 annual sales-division award banquets that are a Schwan's tradition. And as he flies to Texas, New York, New England or California, he studies photographs and memorizes names supplied by the division manager. When he arrives at the banquet, he greets each sales person and his or her spouse by name.

Schwan never seems to tire of those banquets. Every weekend from October through April, he can be found toasting his employees in a Schwan's plant or sales division somewhere in the United States. At each one, he makes a short speech praising employees for their loyalty and reminding them of the preciousness of the free enterprise system.

No employer can remain unaffected when an industrial accident injures one of his people. For Marvin Schwan, the ammonia explosion that occurred in his ice cream plant on August 21, 1981, was particularly devastating. That day, one young worker was killed and five were seriously injured. In the evening, Schwan gathered his closest employees for a meeting that lasted until 11 o'clock. He seemed not to want to leave, Eddie Smith remembers. In subsequent weeks, he made many visits to the injured men in their Twin Cities hospital rooms and to their families.

A man of strong religious beliefs and a champion of close family life, Schwan could not prevent the slow and painful disintegration of his own marriage. Although he handled his divorce with characteristic dignity, he might have faced the alienation of his family and his employees. Instead, he found an outpouring of genuine good wishes when he remarried in October 1981.

□ Marvin Schwan has become a wealthy man, but he knows his priorities. They are, "in order of importance," he says, his religious faith, his family, his country and his business. "And the business provides the money to support the first three." During summers past, his children have taken their places alongside other workers in the Schwan operation. And there is no preferential treatment for the boss's kids.

In many ways, Schwan's empire is an anachronism. While almost every other kind of home delivery system has gone the way of the dinosaur, Schwan's Sales Enterprises has grown and prospered. It has done so, observers agree, because Marvin Schwan has "tended to business," developed a dedicated staff, spread the costs over many products and fine-tuned the sales instrument that is his network of delivery routes.

And it didn't happen overnight.

G.T. Schjeldahl

4

G.T. Schjeldahl

A Life of Pure Events

Gilmore T. Schjeldahl is a complex man. He has been called a creative genius, a restless inventor, a charismatic leader and a corporate maverick—all labels that dismay him. They dismay him not because they are inaccurate, but because they are labels, and labels, he believes, mask reality.

For more than 60 years, Schjeldahl has pursued reality—scientific and technical—in laboratories, on workbenches and in his own mind. A practical man, he recognizes the need for organizations that can turn technological discovery into useful products. For nearly 40 years he has struggled to reconcile two roles: inventor-entrepreneur and corporate executive. One comes as naturally as breathing; the other, he has learned, must eventually be given to someone else, in order to free himself to do what he does best—create new processes and products through chemistry and engineering.

G.T. Schjeldahl is best known for Sheldahl, Inc., the company he founded in 1955. But the Sheldahl Company (originally called the G.T. Schjeldahl Company) was not his first. An earlier venture, Herb-Shelly, was merged with Brown & Bigelow, a St. Paul advertising-products firm, in 1954. Later, in the late 1960s, he founded another corporation, Giltech, to develop machinery for the injection-blow-molding of plastic containers. He merged Giltech with a New Jersey firm when financial troubles threatened to run the company into the ground. Now, as he enters his 70s, he is beginning again, developing a medical device to improve a process known as coronary transluminal angioplasty. This time, he says, he's doing it *without* an organization.

□ Gilmore Schjeldahl grew up in the little North Dakota town of Northwood, near the Red River Valley. It was an ideal place for a young boy with his relentless curiosity about mechanical things. His father, Ole Schjeldahl, knew everything there was to know about steam engines. In the fall, when gigantic threshing machines rolled out across the flat Dakota landscape, Ole had his work cut out for him. It was his job to keep those machines running, and on his rounds he was often accompanied by his towheaded son. The boy loved the noise, the dust, the motion and the excitement of threshing. How could he be afraid, when his dad would give him an oil-can almost as big as he was— and permission to oil anything that moved?

Even before he started school, young Gilmore—or Shelly, as he is known to friends and family—showed an astounding quickness, an ability to understand how complex things worked. But school was another matter. He was inattentive. He daydreamed. He stared out the window. It was even hinted that perhaps he couldn't learn. Once he climbed out of an open first-floor window to follow a trail blazed by his daydreams. His parents wondered what would become of him.

Outside school, Shelly was a different child. He spent hours in an attic workshop, examining anything that had moving parts. He built the family's first radio, stringing a network of antenna wires across the attic for optimum reception. He removed the motor of his mother's Maytag washer for one of his projects. He also became a familiar figure in the shops and businesses of Northwood. He spent hours in the local blacksmith shop, the power plant and the farm-machinery outlet. He ran the movie projector in the local theater. He volunteered his time at the newspaper, where he built a static-eliminator for the press. He helped farmers during harvest.

When the Depression deepened and jobs disappeared, he and four pals set up what they called "South-End Motors" in an abandoned wash-house in one boy's back yard. A burner fueled with used oil kept them warm. "We spent a lot of time arguing and speculating," he remembers. The five built an early version of the snowmobile, complete with a lightweight automobile engine, propeller and wooden skis.

By the time he left Northwood, Schjeldahl had developed a reputation for restlessness, for moving from one job to another. "I grew up something of a renegade," he says. "I had a hard time connecting with anything permanent. If I had been really good at one of those jobs, I'd probably still be in Northwood."

At 21, Schjeldahl enrolled at the North Dakota School of Science at Wahpeton to study electrical-machinery maintenance. But his sister Irene was also in college, and the cost of sending two children to school in those Depression years was more than the Schjeldahls could manage. At a family conference, they decided that Irene would complete her teacher training and Shelly would wait. Instead he joined the Civilian Conservation Corps, a job that others might have considered temporary make-work. He saw it, however, as an opportunity to learn more about the applied engineering that had fascinated him back home. "Nothing I have ever learned has been wasted," Schjeldahl often says. In the CCC he was assigned to the landscape-architecture group planning the International Peace Garden on the North Dakota-Manitoba border. "I was exposed to classic landscape and architectural design," he recalls, "and I picked up civil engineering, photography and surveying skills."

In 1937, Schjeldahl moved to Fargo, where Irene was teaching. He enrolled at North Dakota Agricultural College (now North Dakota State University). Two years later, Irene introduced him to her new roommate, Charlene Hanson, who was a journalism graduate working as a secretary. Schjeldahl's life suddenly came into focus.

One of the few labels Schjeldahl is willing to use identifies phenomena he calls "pure events." A pure event, he says, is a turning-point in a person's life that "locks you

into something important." Like a chemical equation, he
says, a pure event precipitates other events... "and you're
never the same again." Meeting Charlene was one of those
pure events. Within a month he proposed marriage.

Marriage, Schjeldahl knew, meant he had to have a
steady income. He found a job as lab assistant at the Armour & Company packing house in West Fargo. Armour
had just built a new waste-treatment plant, and the company needed someone with a chemistry background to
solve some technical problems. It was grimy work. "I did
everything," Schjeldahl recalls, "from maintaining the
large equipment to doing chemical analyses of the waste.
That job turned out to be a gold mine of information," he
says. It was practical experience that reinforced his study
of biochemistry at college. "If I had not taken that job, I
would have passed up a marvelous education. Besides, it
was the first in a chain of events that led to other opportunities."

Schjeldahl worked at Armour and went to school part-
time for six years. He never did graduate, but he absorbed
information and ideas about chemistry, biology and engineering. In 1943, at the age of 31, he was drafted. The
Army sent him to Virginia Polytechnic Institute—another
opportunity, he says—then to Europe in the infantry.
When victory was declared in Europe, he volunteered for
service in the Pacific in order to get a furlough home to see
Charlene and their two young children. He was guessing
that the war would soon end on the other side of the world
as well, and it did. He never did go to the Pacific.

Instead, Schjeldahl went to Chicago to find work. At
first, he hoped to break into television as a lighting technician. But television lighting, he discovered, was just a matter of throwing switches—no challenge at all. Because he
happened to be in the neighborhood, he stopped one day
at the Armour research laboratories on Chicago's South
Side to see a Mr. Laing, the man to whom all his reports
from West Fargo had been sent.

Americans had a great sense of gratitude for returning
servicemen at that time, he remembers. When Laing asked
what Schjeldahl had been doing since his days in West
Fargo, Schjeldahl pulled out a photograph of himself in
battle dress. "My boy," intoned Laing, "it's not a question of whether or not you will come back to Armour. The

question is, 'What job do you want?' " "They even asked me what salary I thought I should have," Schjeldahl says. "I had made $30 a week before the war, so I asked for $60 —and they agreed!

"I spent the next four days looking at all the job opportunities in the company," Schjeldahl says. He finally chose a meat and meat-byproducts research group working on a project that intrigued him: analyzing the composition of woodsmoke as a tenderizer. But he soon discovered an even more intriguing challenge next door: a pilot plant to freeze and package frozen foods. "When a new packaging material, polyethylene, came along, I became interested in its adaptability to low temperatures," he says. Although polyethylene was pliable and transparent—an ideal material for packaging foods—it stubbornly refused to seal.

On the long commuter-train ride between work and the home he and Charlene had found in Hobart, Indiana, Schjeldahl mulled over the problem. Working evenings in his kitchen on the ideas he generated while riding the train, he developed a means of simultaneously cutting and sealing two sheets of plastic together with a hot knife—a method that would eventually cause a revolution in packaging. At the time, however, another company had cornered the market with a shrink-wrap process called Cryovac, and Schjeldahl's invention lay dormant.

At this impasse, another of Schjeldahl's "pure events" turned his career in a distinctly different direction. A South American who was touring Armour's research facilities went from Schjeldahl's Chicago laboratory to St. Paul, where at a party he met a Twin Cities entrepreneur named Sylvester "Sally" Cargill. Cargill asked the visitor if he'd run across anyone in his travels who knew anything about the new materials called plastics. "I know someone who knows *everything* about plastics!" the visitor replied. Thus, less than a year after he started at Armour, Schjeldahl came to Minneapolis as technical director of Sally Cargill's firm, Associated Activities.

Although Cargill was an ingenious fellow, Schjeldahl recalls, his business methods were somewhat erratic, and their relationship soon began to deteriorate. Schjeldahl decided to use the hot-knife principle he had developed in his Indiana kitchen to set up a bag-making operation in the basement of his south Minneapolis home. He built a machine that was essentially a long, heated knife controlled by a foot pedal, and he secured an order for pickle-barrel liners. "I was pretty near destitute at the time, so when a salesman, Herb Harris, came by and offered to invest $100 in the venture, I was happy to accept. That, plus some money I had saved, was enough to pay for the materials to make up our first order."

Evenings, Schjeldahl turned sheets of plastic into bags in his basement "factory." His mother and mother-in-law folded them upstairs in the kitchen, and on his way to work the next morning, Schjeldahl took the bags downtown to ship them to his customer. "I was having trouble keeping this going," he says with characteristic understatement. "I met a man named Warren Bleeker, a real promoter who had just incorporated his own business in Farmington [Minnesota] and was willing to become a partner." Bleeker and Schjeldahl found two other partners, L.A. Godby and Tom Gaffey, and formed Herb-Shelly, Inc., a company named for Schjeldahl, the president, and for the salesman who had put up the $100. They set up shop in Farmington, and Schjeldahl went looking for another job while Godby ran the bag-making operation.

Schjeldahl was hired by Bemis Brothers Bag Company in St. Paul as manager of its polyethylene packaging development program. Among other inventions, he designed the first air-sickness bag for Northwest Airlines' new Stratocruisers (although that is *not* what he hopes to be remembered for, he says).

Herb-Shelly was attracting some publicity at the time, he remembers, and a Dun & Bradstreet reporter came to the Bemis offices to interview him. Bemis officials began to suspect a conflict of interest, so they fired Schjeldahl. "It was a classic firing," he chuckles. "They took me downstairs, showed me the door, and ushered me through it."

Fortunately, Herb-Shelly was beginning to look like a profitable business, and Schjeldahl could devote full time to the fledgling company's growth. He began looking for capital. He learned the value of high-interest, short-term loans during critical periods from Fred Weil, Sr., of Republic Acceptance Corporation. "I learned that banks are not the only way of financing a company," he says. "You can survive by borrowing money on receivables or inventory. Even if it is a 30 percent loan, if you only need it for a week, it's cheap money."

Schjeldahl made the most of what capital he had. "To stretch my working capital, I would often have my materials shipped to Farmington in the morning, get them off the truck, make up the order and ship it out by about four o'clock. At that time a mail train went through Farmington, so I would quickly make up the invoice, rush over to the depot, mail the letter—with net cash terms—and in three days I'd be on the telephone calling my customer. I'd have my money back in 10 days. I had 30 days on the raw materials, so I'd turn it around at least twice."

Thanks to this kind of fancy footwork, by 1954 Herb-Shelly employed 100 people and had annual sales of approximately $500,000. The company made liners for powdered-milk boxes and bags for freezing foods at home. In addition, Schjeldahl was doing research on Mylar (a flexible, strong polymer created by the DuPont Company), testing its permeability at very thin gauges and developing methods of sealing the polymer with heat and adhesives. He also had a contract with the Office of Naval Research to build experimental atmospheric balloons. Before long, Herb-Shelly attracted the attention of Brown & Bigelow, and in May 1954, Herb-Shelly was acquired as a subsidiary, with Schjeldahl remaining as president.

At Brown & Bigelow, Schjeldahl was viewed as a "crazy inventor," a label that belied his strong business sense and detailed record-keeping as president of Herb-Shelly. He had security and a substantial salary for the mid-1950s— $24,000 a year—but, as he soon realized, "all the money in the world couldn't keep me there." On January 8, 1955, he resigned.

□ Schjeldahl was out of a job again, but he was hardly out of ideas. In fact, he had two good ones: a 125-foot-long machine for sealing polyethylene with heat and a resin capable of sealing Mylar. With an order for a bag-making machine from Continental Can Company, Schjeldahl took the money he had received from the Herb-Shelly merger and on January 21, 1955, went to nearby Northfield, where he found space to build the machine in the pattern shop of a foundry.

For a few months, he operated the new G.T. Schjeldahl Company as sole proprietor. The corporate name was influenced by Forrest Nutting, an investor. When Schjeldahl proposed calling his firm either the Farmington Company or the Premium Bag and Liner Company, Nutting told him to skip the fancy handles. "Put your own name on the line," Nutting said, "and I'll invest."

Schjeldahl eventually found permanent headquarters in the basement of the Medical Arts Building in downtown Northfield. Under the bleachers of the Carleton College football stadium, he worked on a contract for balloons to be used by the University of Minnesota physics department in atmospheric research. He had two employees.

The G.T. Schjeldahl Company balance sheet for 1955 showed $23,745 in assets and $50,187 in liabilities—definitely more promise than profit in both the mechanical (packaging machinery) and polyester film (balloons and heat-sealing adhesive tape) divisions. Schjeldahl realized he needed more funds, so he turned to the venture capital community. Forrest Nutting introduced Schjeldahl to John "Jack" Robinson, chairman of the board of Craig-Hallum, Inc., a Minneapolis investment firm known for backing successful ventures.

Both Robinson and Schjeldahl remember a meeting in the Covered Wagon, a downtown Minneapolis restaurant. "Shelly wanted no more than $50,000 or $60,000, and he wanted to retain complete control of the company," Robinson recalls. "But we knew he needed $200,000 to find out if he had a viable operation." Robinson also insisted that Schjeldahl should not have complete control. "If the creative person has just one percent of the company, he'll stay and produce. The burden is on him to perform, and if problems develop, the other investors can put the pressure on."

It sounded like impending mutiny to Schjeldahl, who had recently been through the Brown & Bigelow merger, in which he'd been, he says, "overwhelmed by money."

"When they told me I needed $200,000 in outside funds, I accused them of trying to overwhelm my venture, to take it away from me," he says. "I almost walked out, but we were in a booth and I was on the inside, so I couldn't." By the end of the meeting, not only had Schjeldahl agreed to the larger amount, he had accepted a minority position.

Then there were some hair-raising moments in the search for capital. Robinson talked three potential investors into driving down to see Schjeldahl's operation for themselves. They went first to the basement factory where Schjeldahl was building his revolutionary packaging machine. "Shelly was in the midst of making some improvements in the machine," Robinson says. "When he started it up to show us how it worked, the gears flew all over the room." Robinson quickly steered the potential investors out to the car and over to Farmington to the drafty warehouse where Schjeldahl had moved the balloon-making operation when the Carleton football season began. There they found the carefully folded balloon fabric shredded by shrews; the animals had been attracted by the cornstarch Schjeldahl had used to keep the fabric from sticking together. *Those* potential investors decided to put their money elsewhere, but Robinson eventually found other backers.

With the infusion of new capital, the Schjeldahl Company began building packaging machinery. Profits increased a healthy 28.5 percent a year, and in 1958, the company, with the help of a local development corporation, moved from its cramped quarters to a new location, dubbed "Schjel-town," on the edge of Northfield.

The company's research in atmospheric balloons had attracted talented people, including Don Piccard, son of pioneer balloonists Jean and Jeannette Piccard. With government contracts for balloon development, the company had truly hitched its wagon to a star. When it was launched in 1960, Schjeldahl's Echo I "satelloon"—made of polyester film fabricated with "Schjel-Bond," the company's adhesive—created a sensation as it made its way around the earth. Newspapers carried schedules of its appearances in the evening skies. Families across the country went out in their back yards to watch that luminous, moving "star," evidence of American progress in space technology.

Two years later, when the first coast-to-coast transmission of a television picture via the orbiting Echo I was accomplished, the G.T. Schjeldahl Company was clearly identified with one of the great adventures of the 20th century. In the next few years the company was involved in more than 20 satellite programs, acquiring valuable technology that was eventually turned into commercial products.

But balloons were not the only use for Schjeldahl's film

and adhesives. Air-supported "Schjel-Domes" were also attention-getters. Lutsen Resort on Lake Superior's North Shore had a covered swimming pool where guests basked in summery temperatures under a Schjeldahl bubble—surrounded outside by snow-covered trees. A luminous domed real estate office stopped night-time traffic in suburban St. Louis Park, Minnesota. And, in Northfield, the company erected the "Schjel-Mile," a 540-foot-long, air-supported factory building. Not surprisingly, the domes and the satellites captured the public's imagination, and Schjeldahl became known as a small company with a big future. The company was barely seven years old, but its founder was already thinking of the next technological frontier.

□ "In 1960, I started attending seminars in microcircuitry," Schjeldahl says. "By 1963, I had identified this market, and we were building experimental equipment. I planned a meeting in New York to talk about opportunities in microcircuitry with the investment community—and a couple of people on my board were horrified. They thought I had no business talking about something the company really didn't have."

The dynamic tension between the creative individual and his more "practical" investors can be difficult to maintain. It was a winning combination for the G.T. Schjeldahl Company for a number of years, but inevitably there were problems. "At first, I was running a horizontal organization," Schjeldahl says. "I was president, chairman of the board and treasurer. I had a small board, but we did begin adding some people in 1961." One new board member was Paul Garrett, retired chief of public relations for General Motors. Another was Richard G. Brierly, then vice president of The Drackett Company of Cincinnati. The other directors were A.C. Smith, Jr., an attorney; Jack Robinson of Craig-Hallum, and D.M. Winton of Minneapolis. Forrest Nutting, one of the original directors, died in 1961.

The clash of opinion about the company's direction that surfaced in 1963 would become near-cacophony before the decade's end. The board began insisting the company should have more sophisticated management. Because he recognized his own limitations, Schjeldahl agreed. He began broadening the management structure and hired Arthur J. Hatch, an engineer-consultant, as executive vice president in 1964. He sent two employees, Richard Slater (now senior vice president in charge of new ventures) and James Womack (now president and chief executive officer) to Harvard University's Advanced Management Program for Executives.

It was a turbulent period. In its early years, the company was made up of employees hand-picked and motivated by Schjeldahl himself. One of those was Slater, who has been with the company since 1955. "Shelly never let us think there were any limitations," Slater recalls. "He made us believe we could move mountains. And he had a knack for turning failure into success. 'A failure causes us to re-think the problem,' he would say. 'Now we're much further ahead than we would have been if we hadn't had the failure.'

"Shelly was always at work before anyone else," Slater continues. "It became a game to see if we could get here before he did. Sometimes, when we were working on a problem, he would get up in the middle of the night, come down here and sweep up. It helped him think. He was extremely persistent—like a bulldog—but he could be unpredictable, too. Sometimes, when things weren't going right, he'd come along and sweep everything into the garbage can so everyone would have to start over."

There was no doubt in the company that Schjeldahl was a visionary. "He had fascinating ideas," says Richard Brierly, now chairman of the company's board. "But sometimes his ideas ran faster than he could express them. He would start to explain something he wanted to do, and his mind would work so fast that he would just leave the rest of us behind. Sometimes he had trouble getting normal people to see as far ahead as he can see."

In 1963, the company "stubbed its toe" when sales did not increase markedly from the previous year and net income actually declined. The next year, Schjeldahl acquired a paper-bag-making machine division of the St. Regis Paper Company and moved its entire packaging division to Providence, Rhode Island. By 1964, profits were up again and the company was, for the time being, on a steadier course. Still, the differences between Schjeldahl and his directors widened.

Schjeldahl decided that Arthur Hatch, the executive vice

president he had just hired, should become president immediately. "I was moving faster than the board thought I should," he recalls, "but they went along with it. I saw the future in new fields and figured that if I could divest myself of day-to-day management, I could move faster in other areas. Besides, things were going well. We had a huge price-earnings ratio, I had about four million in personal wealth, and I wanted to pursue new ideas."

So Schjeldahl relinquished the reins to Hatch, while retaining his position as chairman of the board. The company began concentrating on growth in the electrical products division—taking technology that wasn't fully developed, a wary Schjeldahl believed, and bringing in professional management too early. The board committed the company to a 25 percent annual increase in sales and profits and a 20 percent return on shareholders' equity, a goal that Schjeldahl saw as disastrous. "If you spend your time doing what you do best, growth will take care of itself," he argued.

Schjeldahl felt more and more isolated and unused. His projects—research in new areas with potential—were pushed aside. In 1966, he resigned as chairman, though he was still a corporate employee. Then the board took an action that seemed to him to demonstrate a complete lack of faith. He had an employment agreement that included a termination clause specifying a six-month notice. The board removed the six-month clause so that his contract could terminate automatically and the issue of his employment would just not come up. "It would have been a vote of confidence," he says. "I wanted the board to take a position." The board didn't.

"It was an upsetting period," one board member says. "Instead of facing the problems immediately and directly, we had a series of crises. We felt the company had become too large for Shelly to run in an orderly way. We were in a transition period—all of us recognized the symptoms—but we hadn't worked out a clear-cut way of making the changes we needed. Every member on the board admired Shelly, felt he had much to contribute. But we felt his role had to be redefined, that he couldn't operate as he had in the past. The termination-clause issue was used as a way to communicate a change. Unfortunately, we used crises and symbols to deal with one another rather than talking things through.''

Schjeldahl removed himself completely from the company he had founded just 10 years earlier. He established another enterprise, Giltech Development Company, to pursue the market for the injection-blow-molding of containers made from polymeric materials—pharmaceutical and beverage containers. But he was not away from the G.T. Schjeldahl Company for long.

In 1966-67, the company slipped badly, and Schjeldahl was asked to return as board chairman. The company had over-committed itself, making shipments at any cost. ''The scrap rate was so high that the selling price for some products didn't even cover the cost of materials,'' Schjeldahl says. To make matters worse, a down-turn in the economy made those 25 percent growth projections sheer fantasy.

One of Schjeldahl's first duties was to persuade Art Hatch to resign. Another board member conducted extensive interviews with all the people who reported to Hatch. ''It became clear that Art was so motivated, and so committed to his notion of how to run the company, that his people were telling him only what they thought he wanted to hear,'' the board member says. Schjeldahl later learned that another executive had worked to undermine Hatch by channeling information behind Hatch's back. Hatch resigned, and George Freeman, who had been vice president and treasurer, assumed operational responsibilities. It was a trying time for all concerned, ''the most emotional thing I've ever been through,'' says Hatch. ''I trusted too many people—particularly three or four who used me as a target when they saw the opportunity to move themselves up in the company.''

Under George Freeman, the company had three rocky years. Sales declined by almost $4 million in 1968, and the company recorded a net loss of $742,000. The picture brightened in 1969, but in 1970 the company again recorded losses. The company eventually regained its equilibrium, thanks to the toughness of Jim Womack, Schjeldahl says. Womack turned the packaging machinery division around and was later (in 1971) made president of the company.

In 1969, Schjeldahl left the company again—this time to attend to new problems. ''Just as I was going public with my new venture, Giltech, the equity recession occurred. By

1970, my $4 million had dropped to a negative net worth, and I needed additional capital to develop my machine." At the same time, G.T. Schjeldahl Company stock hit bottom.

Schjeldahl found a merger partner for Giltech in the Rainville Company, Inc., of Middlesex, New Jersey. "Rainville agreed to manufacture my machine in exchange for the right to buy Giltech. I closed down my operation in Golden Valley [a Minneapolis suburb] and saw that my 10 employees had other jobs." Through a manufacturing contract and his own consulting work in plastics, he was able to pay off creditors. He became chairman of the board at Rainville and set about rebuilding his fortune, acquiring patents as he went along.

Through the years, Schjeldahl has retained an interest in the Sheldahl Company (the "c" and the "j" were dropped for convenience of spelling), although he is not a part of its operations. He still holds about 2.3 percent of the company's outstanding stock, and he has continued to offer advice through the years, "most of it unsolicited," he says. He says that he is still "extremely proud" of the company and its managers. Furthermore, the spirit of inquiry he established during the firm's formative years remains.

After some turbulent years in the 1970s, the Sheldahl Company began a steady resurgence, consolidating its product line and eliminating, eventually, the packaging machinery division that had been the basis for early growth. The company's sales for fiscal 1981 were $34.5 million.

☐ In 1978, Gilmore Schjeldahl suffered an angina attack. While he was being treated at Hennepin County Medical Center, he began quizzing physicians about treatment methods for cardiac disease. He learned of a procedure called transluminal angioplasty, in which a small, plastic, balloon-tipped catheter is used to compress built-up plaque that threatens to block coronary arteries. Schjeldahl saw an opportunity to use his knowledge of plastics and their properties to make a better catheter. He began, again, the painstaking and exhilarating process of developing a product and organizing a corporation. This time, he chose the name Cathedyne. And this time, Schjeldahl is working virtually alone. He has one assistant in his Minnetonka laboratory; most of the work is sub-contracted to others.

Schjeldahl realizes, however, that no entrepreneurial effort is a solo endeavor. "You never really accomplish something by yourself," he says. "No matter what your plans are, there's always someone who's better skilled. If you can get that person's services, you're better for it. I learned not to become snarled in one person's limitations. I set up multiple channels; I have two almost identical sets of work going on in different places. I choose the one I think is best—but I don't abandon the other. I may have that other person work on a different part of the project. I stop in to make sure they're moving along; some I see as often as twice a day, some once a week, others once or twice a month. As long as they are working on it, the project will reach an end."

Schjeldahl proceeds deliberately. "We sometimes think that it's better to do something than just stand still. But there are times when doing nothing is better. If you take off in the wrong direction, it might be disastrous. In most organizations, people are pushed to act before thinking things through.

"I try to single out what's important," he continues. "I try not to deal with trivial things, and I avoid doing something just to be busy. The times I've gotten into trouble were the times when I had to do something just to assuage my anxiety."

Those who have known Schjeldahl through the years recognize him as a man with great ability to focus on a project. "He marches to his own drummer," says a colleague. "He doesn't seem to need support for his ideas from people around him. He works harder than anyone else—but he's enthusiastic, and he has fun at what he's doing."

Others speak of Schjeldahl's inquiring and disciplined mind. They say he perseveres, he believes nothing is impossible, he is unwilling to accept defeat. He meticulously documents every conversation, every discovery, no matter what project he happens to be working on. His files contain hundreds of small spiral-bound notebooks, restaurant napkins and placemats with drawings and notes that summarize a life of inquiry. His view of money is utilitarian. "Money is a means of accomplishing what I want to do." Confronted with a roomful of money and a roomful of ideas, he says, he would choose the ideas.

G.T. Schjeldahl is both entrepreneur and inventor. But he maintains the two are not the same. "The entrepreneur acquires people and money to help the inventor work through ideas. In my experience, the two roles are almost mutually exclusive." His old friend Jack Robinson, however, says that Schjeldahl is both entrepreneur and inventor—and, in addition, a conceptual thinker. Robinson likens human intelligence to a wheel. "Most people have 'spoke' intelligence," he explains. "But really creative people—and I've only known six or eight in my lifetime—have 'rim' intelligence that comprehends connections and can put together unrelated facts and ideas. They can also project into the future."

Robinson remembers a classic Schjeldahl statement made during one particularly heated investors' meeting. "Don't bother me with details," Schjeldahl said. "I think in conclusions."

Louis Cosentino

5

Louis Cosentino

'Doing Something Right'

A hospital treatment center for kidney disease seems an unlikely inspiration for a young entrepreneur. But when Louis Cosentino, a transplanted New Yorker with a new Ph.D. and an impressive string of patents to his credit, saw kidney dialysis in operation for the first time, he knew he had work to do.

It was 1972, and Cosentino, age 28, had just become director of advanced research and development at Medtronic, Inc., the world's leading manufacturer of cardiac pacemakers. Cosentino's job was to diversify the company, and that first glimpse of dialysis clearly showed an opportunity for improving treatment methods in another area of medicine.

What Louis Cosentino saw at the Regional Kidney Disease Program in Minneapolis in 1972 is a way of life for 60,000 Americans whose lives depend on dialysis. Three times a week, for four to six hours, they must be connected to artificial kidneys. Two large needles are inserted in the patient's arm, and blood is pumped through one needle and an attached tube to the artificial kidney or dialyzer, where it is cleansed, and pumped back to the body through the other needle. It is a painful and costly treatment, but without it those people with failed kidneys would die.

Cosentino and a half-dozen bio-engineers in his department at Medtronic began making plans to work cooperatively with Dr. Fred Shapiro, head of the regional kidney program. In a few weeks, they were trained as dialysis technicians, connecting patients to kidney machines, learning how the treatment worked and how the patients reacted.

At Medtronic, a marketing study confirmed the need for better equipment and a ready market. Bolstered by the enthusiasm of his department, Cosentino presented a research plan to Medtronic's top-level management—only to have it rejected in 1974 as too far afield from cardiac pacing and Medtronic's origins.

Disappointed, Cosentino told Dr. Shapiro that they wouldn't be able to work together after all. Dr. Shapiro said: "Lou, why don't you start your own company?" And Cosentino replied: "Sure, Fred. All it takes is a million dollars."

☐ Within a few weeks, however, Louis Cosentino had $700,000 in financing, a rented building and plans for a new company underway. Because his purpose was to make products for treating patients with kidney disease, he named the company Renal Systems, Inc. For Cosentino, it was the right field of medicine. Without a doubt, he had around him the people who could help make dramatic improvements in kidney treatment. But before he began, he went to Earl Bakken, Medtronic's founder and chairman. "I told him I would not compete with Medtronic, and I would not take any people from the pacemaker business," Cosentino recalls. "I told him I wanted to improve kidney treatment, and he wished me well."

None of the 26 researchers he had brought to Medtronic knew what Cosentino was about to do. He quietly resigned his job and placed a "help wanted" ad in the local Sunday paper. By the end of the next week, he had a company with a staff of eight, including himself—all former members of the advanced research and development department at Medtronic. Together, they painted and remodeled the Minneapolis warehouse that would be the new company's headquarters. They built research benches and dreamed of the future. Their first product, they decided, would be the saline concentrate used to cleanse patients' blood. They bought mixing tanks, put them in place, poured concrete and laid pipes—eight young engineers building their company from scratch.

"It was an exciting time for us," Cosentino remembers. "Each of the men had a piece of the company. The company was theirs. It seemed there was nothing we couldn't do—especially when that first batch of concentrate was made and we had a product."

Cosentino himself was the first salesman. Packed up and sent to Chicago, making four or five calls a day, he saw every kidney-treatment facility there within a week. "I told them about our company, what a wonderful science department we had, and what great things we were going to do in the kidney field," he says. "And I asked them to please buy our product because we needed the business."

The enthusiasm of Cosentino's partners during those early months is testimony to his ability to gain others' confidence. In part, that confidence was grounded in his mechanical and engineering abilities, and those abilities had surfaced early in his life.

Cosentino was born in Brooklyn in 1944. His father, an industrial oil-burner mechanic, recognized his son's talents; the younger Cosentino's first memories are of working beside his dad, exploring the mysteries of machines and electrical appliances. "I learned common sense from my father," he says. "We always looked for ways to make things simpler. He taught me not to be afraid to tackle anything. We may not always have been successful, but there wasn't anything mechanical we were afraid to take apart. He taught me to believe that if someone else had put a machine together, I could take it apart and put it back together again."

The basement of the family home became the workshop where Louis and his younger brother Jerry learned the inner workings of television sets, radios and various other household appliances. By age 15, Louis could not only repair toasters and washing machines, he could lay bricks and concrete, do carpentry work and electrical wiring—all of that in addition to school work, sand-lot baseball and his favorite pastime, fishing from the Brooklyn piers.

Although Louis Cosentino Sr. trained his sons well, he had one goal: that they go to college—and have jobs that did *not* require working with their hands.

Graduating from a technical high school at 16, Louis Cosentino entered Polytechnic Institute of Brooklyn to study engineering and become a computer technician, a repairman or programmer. In his junior year, he applied for a part-time job in the school's new biomedical engineering lab where he met a teacher who would profoundly influence his life.

Dr. Jesse Crump is a softspoken Midwesterner, a medical doctor and an electrical engineer. He remembers Lou Cosentino as a "disillusioned electrical engineering student who caught fire" when he discovered biological engineering and physical chemistry. In long informal sessions, Cosentino and other students would press Dr. Crump for information about human physiology and anatomy. "We asked him all sorts of questions," Cosentino recalls. "How does a lung work? How does a kidney work? How does a cell work? He would answer our questions hour after hour. When he didn't have the answer, he would say so, and that made us even more curious." It was Dr. Crump and this newly formed bio-engineering department that sparked Cosentino's interest in medicine.

When Cosentino began working on a master's degree, Dr. Crump became his advisor. "In research, Lou could spot problems no one else saw," he remembers. "He had a very creative mind and could think of unusual solutions to those problems, solutions that often combined several technologies."

☐ As he neared the end of his master's program, Lou Cosentino had to make a decision. He was encouraged to continue his education to become a researcher. In academia, he recalls, industry was not a popular word, and students received little practical training. Instead, they learned theory—and were trained to think and solve problems. But Louis Cosentino was ready to apply his theoretical training. "I knew I wanted to be an engineer, even though I wasn't sure what engineers did. I *knew* what researchers did, because I worked at research all day long." He decided to leave the academic world for industry, and his first job was with Hoffman-La Roche, a large pharmaceutical company with facilities in New Jersey.

Hoffman-La Roche, it turned out, was as much an institution as Brooklyn Poly, with laboratories that were a researcher's paradise. It seemed an ideal setting for a talented engineer, yet Cosentino found his hope to achieve tangible results unmet. "I was asked to do research in electrodes and brain studies, and I became what might be called a publication factory. The department head would discuss an idea with me, I would go to the lab, and six to eight months later we would have a publication. There were no products—and there was no financial accountability. It was frustrating because what I was doing didn't seem useful."

His company entered a joint venture with RCA to create medical products. Combining the research departments of the two companies proved difficult, and Cosentino found himself with little direction and increasing disillusionment about working for a large company. He spent more and more time in the lab inventing devices, a response to adversity that would become his trademark, and he grew increasingly impatient. When Hoffman-La Roche acquired RCA's electronics division and Cosentino learned he would be reporting to a manager from RCA, he decided he'd had enough. "But I didn't want to leave without saying my piece," he says. "I wrote a letter to the president of Hoffman-La Roche, telling him what I believed were the major problems in the medical-electronics division. They had a fine company, but the management was ineffective, and I couldn't stand to waste any more time with them."

Cosentino then became chief engineer for Datascope, a small New Jersey company, where he designed products and supervised manufacturing. He had gone from pure research to practical, hands-on engineering, and he realized he was unprepared. "I failed miserably at Datascope. I just wasn't ready," he says. "After a few months, I got a call from the head of my division at Hoffman-La Roche— offering to hire me back, with two days a week off to go to school." Later he learned that the company's president had asked to have him re-hired.

Back at Hoffman-La Roche, Cosentino found himself working with senior engineers from RCA, several of whom had helped develop television in the late 1940s and early

1950s. "I spent hours, days—months—with those engineers," he recalls. "With nearly every idea I came up with, one of them would pull a design out of a desk drawer and say, 'Hey, I did that in 1952.' The division's management hadn't improved that much, but I didn't care because I was learning." Given special research projects, he was left alone to invent devices and turn out patents.

Cosentino picked up more than engineering skills in those years at Hoffman-La Roche. "I learned that marketing in the medical field is very simple: If the product is useful, it will sell, and if it isn't useful, it won't. Lots of large companies have tried to get into this field, have made honest investments and have fallen on their faces. They build products that are too expensive or apply to only a limited number of patients—and they spend too much money doing it. They just don't have the right people to create the right products."

The years he spent at Hoffman-La Roche and Datascope were years of hard work for Cosentino. He worked during the day and went to school at night, earning a doctorate in bio-engineering. Fortunately, he had a partner: Lou and Judi Cosentino were married at 21, after knowing each other since the age of 12. As teenagers, they had planned together to make their mark on the world. Both say they have been best friends virtually all their lives. While Lou worked on a master's degree, Judi taught school. Later, when they began making plans for Renal Systems, it was Judi who searched for a building for the new company. Then, expecting their third child, she was confident through months of uncertain income. "No matter what happens," she remembers telling friends, "we'll still have each other. And if I can't bet on Lou, I can't bet on anything." Today her talents are evident in the company's promotional materials; she designs and produces all product brochures and advertisements.

In 1972, after five years of study, Lou Cosentino received his doctorate. A former colleague at Hoffman-La Roche offered him a job with Medtronic, the Minnesota pacemaker company. But Cosentino had had enough of big companies, he decided, and besides, he was thinking of starting out on his own. Still, when Medtronic officials persuaded him to come west for a look, he agreed. "Judi and I had been working hard for five years, so we decided to go to Minnesota just for a weekend—even though our roots and our families were in New York and we had no intention of moving away." Arriving in January, in below-zero temperatures, the couple was whisked in a warm automobile to Medtronic facilities. Cosentino liked what he saw. By the time the weekend was over, both Lou and Judi knew they would be moving to Minneapolis.

At Medtronic, Cosentino began immediately to build an advanced research department with the best engineering talent he could find. He brought in 26 men, all with advanced degrees and all young, bright and talented. Two years later, seven of those engineers would become the nucleus of Renal Systems, Inc.

☐ In its first years, Cosentino's new company had its share of problems. Renal Systems was born during the 1974 recession. The oil embargo didn't help, either; sodium acetate, a petroleum product and an essential ingredient in saline concentrate, was supplied by only one U.S. firm, and the young company was told it would receive no allocation at all. Only persistent telephone calls—starting with the supplier company's president—enabled production of the concentrate to begin.

The delay in supplies was just the beginning. Even though the company had a product and was making sales, profits were elusive. "We looked at everything we were doing," Cosentino says, "and the only unknown factor was the cost of shipping the concentrate. So we decided to rent a truck and ship it ourselves. A Texan came in to apply for a job wearing a cowboy hat and boots. We asked him if he could drive a truck, and when he said yes we told him to rent one and go to Chicago. He had no idea how to get to Chicago, but we sent him out anyway. That was the beginning of our shipping department. I was told it wasn't possible to have your own trucks and ship at a lower cost than the freight companies could, but we did it. We lease trucks, and now we have the best mileage figures—possibly the best safety record—in the fleet. We're still the only company in our field to have its own trucks."

Renal Systems then began to develop more complex electronic products for kidney dialysis. A dialysate meter that clinicians use to measure proper mixing of saline solution required the machining of small parts, Lee Fischback, one of the first employees, remembers. "We didn't have time to wait for parts ordered from a supplier to be sent out to us, to be checked for accuracy and to be possibly returned for further work," Fischback says. "So we bought a mill and a box of tools, and began making our own. It was painstaking work—sometimes Lou and I would spend hours making one cut 1/1,000th of an inch deep."

The dialysate meter under way, Renal Systems began manufacturing a device to detect possible air bubbles in blood as it passes through tubing to the dialysis machine. Like other companies, Renal Systems' air-leak detector used infrared light. But at a trade show, Cosentino met a competitor who claimed his product could detect certain clinical conditions Renal Systems' product could not. As Cosentino recalls, "I came back from the show, took our device into the lab to test it, and, sure enough, they were right—our product did not detect that set of clinical conditions. I wanted to pull it off the market—it wasn't the best and therefore not up to our standards—and re-design it. But we were pressed financially, and our board did not agree."

The device functioned well, and there was slim chance of danger to the patients. It seemed certain the product would not be changed. Cosentino, however, refused to give up. "I announced that the company had me from nine in the morning to five in the afternoon, but after five I could do what I wanted to do, and I wanted to re-design that product." Working evenings, Cosentino and Fischback re-designed the bubble detector, using ultrasound instead of infrared light, and completed the design in 30 days. Within six months, Renal Systems' air-bubble detector had captured the market. "If it weren't for that product," Cosentino now says, "we might not be in business today."

In 1976, two years after its founding, Renal Systems found itself in a crisis many young businesses face: increased production costs caused by rapidly increasing sales create a severe shortage of cash—a manufacturer's nightmare. "You buy raw materials from suppliers, and they have to be paid in 30 days. But *you* don't get paid by customers for 90 days. The more you sell, the more you must build, and the more cash you need to keep going," Cosentino explains. "It becomes a vicious circle. If you don't have a way to finance your receivables, you can't pay the suppliers, first for 60 days and then for 90 days. Then they cut you off, and you can't manufacture. When you can't manufacture, you can't make any money. A viable company can actually outgrow itself.

"It was a shock to all of us," he says. "The better we did, the worse it got. We went to the banks, but the business environment was bad and money was tight. They refused to lend us money—they said we were too risky. So a friend who had raised much of the initial capital for the company raised another $125,000 privately—and we consumed that in less than 30 days. We knew we had to have a bank. Bob Rosner, our executive vice president, went to Northwestern Bank, with the backing of Amos Heilicher [a Minneapolis businessman], and again tried to make arrangements. Finally, Amos guaranteed the loan for two months. Without that help we would have gone under.

"The day came when I just sat behind my desk knowing it was out of my hands. You can't pressure the banks, you just have to wait. So I went to the lab and began doing the only thing I could—inventing new devices."

Cosentino's determination to re-design the air-leak detector and to find funds to continue operations is characteristic. He persists. He also refuses to believe that what he wants to do cannot be done. As he began to study the effects of dialysis on patients' health, he suspected that the polyvinyl chloride commonly used for tubing might leach toxic materials into the blood that passes through it. "Lou decided that urethane would be safer," Dr. Fred Shapiro recalls. "But urethane is extremely difficult to work with—it's either too stiff or too soft—and it is prohibitively expensive."

Only Cosentino believed urethane could be used. He developed a method of co-extruding the tubing in two layers, vinyl on the outside and urethane on the inside. "We hired a company that was supposed to be the expert in making plastic tubing," he says. "They built a co-extrusion system for us, and we tried to make it work for almost a year. At the end of the year, that company told us it couldn't be done. But I wouldn't give up. I had to make it work." Re-designing the extrusion process himself, he eventually did make it work—although it was, he admits, a long, painful and expensive process.

"It took us almost four years to straighten out all the

problems, and it is difficult to do that when you have an ongoing operation. You are short on research people and capital—you can't just go out and buy $100,000 worth of tools at once. The injection molds we have took three years to build, and each one corrected a major problem—in assembly, in cost, in production."

☐ What do Lou Cosentino's colleagues say makes him a successful entrepreneur? Many speak of his decisiveness. "He's not afraid to make a decision and act on it," says one. "And he's perceptive. He has a sixth sense that enables him to see today what will be happening five years from now. He's also a terrific engineer. He knows what technology is available. He decides what the product will be, then he finds a way to make it. And he doesn't limit himself to the way things have always been done."

Another associate speaks of Cosentino's confidence in his own ideas. He has a drive to accomplish, and it often means accomplishing what he's told cannot be done. He believes nothing is impossible. "He won't give up," the associate says. "The tougher things become, the harder and longer he works."

Others describe Cosentino's continual effort to educate himself through reading and his ability to recall ideas and technologies over long periods of time. "The man is a walking library," says an employee.

Employees say Cosentino has a personal, informal way of managing people. "He accommodates everyone's style," says one. "Some of us work quickly, while others may make decisions based on numbers and drawn-out analysis. Lou accommodates all of us. I don't think I have ever worked for anyone like him. It is enjoyable, fulfilling—and at times outrageously frustrating. But I wouldn't be here if I wasn't having a good time. Lou is brilliant, he's fun, he's hard but fair."

"In many ways, his strengths are also his weaknesses," says still another employee. "His certainty that nothing is impossible can be carried to extremes—he won't let go or say 'enough.' Somehow, he has both a broad and a narrow way of viewing his work. He knows where he wants the company to go, and his vision is broad and real. But it's difficult for him to formulate a step-by-step plan. He relies on others to provide the details. At the same time, his vision can be narrow: he often doesn't see the implications of staying with a project too long."

Cosentino also has the ability to change. As one of his managers says, "Lou was a New Yorker, but he became a Midwesterner, with a Midwesterner's way of doing business. When he started, he was a scientist—a mad scientist—and he became a businessman."

Cosentino's pace and high expectations have had their casualties, to be sure. Of the seven men who helped him found the company, only one remains. But he has learned, over the years, that he can't expect from others the kind of near-fanatic dedication he demands of himself. The persistence, however, remains.

In 1981, Renal Systems, with sales of more than $10 million, introduced two new products. One, a "blood-access device," was the first of Renal Systems' devices to attract venture capital for research and development—$1 million from several individuals and institutions. Long-awaited by patients, the Hemasite shunt is implanted under the skin and permits dialysis without the large needles that bruise patients' arms and damage their veins. Another new product, a machine that cleanses dialyzers so they can be re-used, means significant savings for the treatment centers. Products that enable them to economize without diminishing patient care are doubly useful.

Both devices represent advances in dialysis, just what Lou Cosentino intended when he founded Renal Systems. "My goal," Cosentino says, "is to help other people. I recognized that the way to accomplish that goal was to make products, rather than to provide a service or do basic research. The company's goal is to improve the health and care of the kidney dialysis patient. I needed the company to get done what I wanted to do. I didn't start this company because I wanted to go into business for myself. I started it because I wanted to invent and make devices, and I was not able to do it the way I wanted to within another company."

Cosentino has a second goal: to make Renal Systems the premier company in dialysis products. Not the biggest necessarily, but the best. "Our method is to acquire and harness technology to make useful products for a specific area of medicine," he explains.

Like most entrepreneurs, Cosentino is an optimist. He

also loves his work. "Work is fun," he insists. "It's not a chore. I enjoy thinking about it, discussing my problems, and I always enjoy coming to work. When it stops being fun, well, then it's time to quit."

He also recognizes the importance of taking calculated risks. "If you really want to start a business, there is nothing that will stop you. But you have to be willing to take the financial risk—your house and your car—personally. If you fail you just start over again. People who try to solve all the problems before they start never seem to get started."

Cosentino is, by his own admission, a dreamer. On long flights, when others read, he sketches and talks about ideas for advances in medical engineering. "There are things I would like to make, things that have always fascinated me," he muses. "Someday someone will find the key to what makes individual cells grow into hearts, kidneys and all the other parts of the body. If we could figure that out, we could grow organs—any part of the body we wanted to. And we know for sure that it can be done because it happens millions of times a day. Eventually failed or diseased organs will be replaced by *new* ones, not artificial ones, and there will be no rejection problems."

Cosentino's experience in large corporations clearly shaped the way he manages employees within his own company. He believes in being accessible to his 200 employees. Sleeves rolled up, he can be found in the production or research areas as often as he is in his own office. "In most companies, the hourly people view the people in the front office as the 'shirts,' " he says. "When a company grows, bad feeling can develop between the two. I believe the people in the back are just as important as the people in the front offices. You just can't succeed unless everyone is pulling together. We all have something important to do here."

All management people at Renal Systems, including the president, have manned production lines. "Many people in the company know I have done their jobs and could do them again if I had to," says Cosentino. "I have been beside them for many hours, doing some pretty heavy work. They know I appreciate what they do, and they appreciate me. So it's easier for them to talk to me, and if I ask them to do something extra, they'll pitch in and help."

☐ Despite his devotion to his business, Cosentino is keenly aware of his role as husband and father of four. Although there are times when he works 16 hours a day, seven days a week, sometimes for a month at a time, he does not seem to be an absent father. In many ways, Judi Cosentino is responsible for the family's unity. Work has always been an important part of their lives, and the couple shares the sense of purpose that propels Cosentino and his company.

In 1980, Cosentino received recognition for his accomplishment. He was nominated as one of Minnesota's Ten Outstanding Young Men by the Junior Chamber of Commerce in Plymouth, the Minneapolis suburb that is his home and the location of his company. Later that year, he was chosen by the national Junior Chamber of Commerce as one of the Ten Outstanding Young Men in the country. In Tulsa, Oklahoma, he and his family sat in a great hall, watching a slide presentation that reviewed his life and achievements. It was, says Judi Cosentino, as if people were saying, for the first time, "You're doing something right."

William Norris

6

William Norris

'There Ain't No Backin' Up'

It was duty, not magnetism, that pulled William Norris back to the family farm in 1932. What had once been productive acreage in southern Nebraska was now barren. Bone-dry soil cracked, then billowed through the air in dust clouds. There was no feed to keep the hogs and cattle alive. Debts seemed to multiply geometrically. That spring, Mildred Norris became a widow, left to run the flagging farm alone in the Depression, the drought and the threat of flood from the nearby Republican River. Her only son had to come back.

At 21, William Norris was one month away from graduation when his father collapsed with a heart attack. Norris scrambled to complete his engineering coursework at the University of Nebraska early. At least he would return with a degree and a future with more security.

William Norris had lived with farming's agonizing variables all his life, but he had not come to accept them. The only way to save the farm, he reasoned, was to keep the cattle alive. The market had plummeted, but cattle still brought $12, maybe $14 a head. In a household that had seen its resources dwindle to $5, cattle was the only hope. Other farmers in Webster County had been forced to sell their starving herds and finally surrendered everything to the bank. The Norris farm would not be surrendered to anyone.

Dry grassland would keep the cattle on a subsistence diet until fall, but winter threatened starvation. Norris remembered an episode from childhood. When he fed the cattle green alfalfa hay in winters past, the steers poked through it and picked out the Russian thistle. It was a useless plant, growing wild in the fields, but Norris steers had an appetite for it.

In an enterprise saturated with convention, William Norris did the unconventional. He would cut the thistle growing wild, store it and feed it to the cattle all winter. Neighbors thought Norris had lost his mind. He couldn't even find help harvesting the thistle because no self-respecting farmer—even a destitute one—would be caught saving thistle for feed. It simply wasn't done. Feed those cattle thistle, and they'll probably die or wind up cross-eyed by spring, the locals said. The Norris kid was crazy to think he could keep a herd alive on useless weeds.

Norris' cattle lost weight over the winter, but they bore healthy calves and not a single one died.

When the spring of 1933 came, it finally rained. Norris was over the hump. He could market his livestock and put the fields back to work. He had done what he had to.

But William Norris didn't stay on the farm. He left Nebraska in 1934 to embark on a career light-years away from farming—a career that eventually led to Control Data, now 141st among *Fortune* magazine's prominent 500, a corporation with 60,000 employees in 47 countries, pulling in at least $4.2 billion annually and ranking among the top five computer companies worldwide.

Yet Norris is not so far from the farm he was anxious to leave five decades ago. He learned lessons in entrepreneurship, pragmatism and resourcefulness there. Where else does a kid begin to build empires with baling wire? Where else does he learn to coax—or command—a mule into doing things his way? Where else does he learn about natural cycles, about variables beyond his control, about cash flow and creative financing?

William Norris took what he learned on a thousand

acres in southern Nebraska and applied those lessons to a multinational corporation in Minnesota.

☐ Norris was a twin. He and his sister Willa started life together in 1911 on the then-prosperous Norris farm. They grew up sharing farm chores and money-making schemes. Grandad Daniel Norris, a first-generation farmer on that land, had "retired" to tend apple and cherry orchards nearby. There was money in picking the fruit. Not only that, the Nebraska prairie was wild with skunk, civet cat, badger and squirrel. Willa and William set traps and pulled in good money for the animal skins—enough to buy a handful of $25 and $50 savings bonds in the 1920s.

When William was not doing farm chores, picking fruit or trapping, he was holed up in his room making ham radio contact with distant voices. Norris and W9ASR ("You can't get those short call letters anymore," Norris, today at 71, says with genuine delight) reached far beyond Webster County through the magic of radio. His room was decorated with *Popular Mechanics*, vacuum tubes, copper wire and Zane Grey tales of the Wild West. His walls were papered with postcards and call letters identifying his radio compatriots. The postcards were like a prized collection of baseball cards, only Norris talked to every one in his collection. No one had a set precisely like his.

Norris pored over electronics magazines, ordering radio parts and gadgets. His parents wondered if he could pay for them, and sometimes he couldn't. But Mildred and William Sr. made up the difference, believing their son's forays into science might eventually serve him well. "Our parents believed," Willa says, "that he knew more about physics than the high school physics teacher." Several years later, Norris paid a man for a two-year subscription to the *Saturday Evening Post* with two live chickens. The Depression had struck, and the family was down to a few dollars. "He got a couple dinners," Norris, the insatiable reader, argued, "but we have 24 months of good material."

Willa and William walked or rode a pony, in all weather, to a one-room schoolhouse about a mile from their home.

"William and Willa," the teacher had said sweetly, "and who is older?"

"I am," William volunteered, "...by two minutes."

He may have been first, but he wasn't the best student. Willa always pulled better grades. "I studied," she says, "and Bill didn't. I always believed that he had more natural brainpower than I."

In high school, while William Norris distinguished himself in math and physics, he was not exactly a flash on the football field. In the first game of his first season, he fractured a bone in his knee. "He just didn't have the football physique," Willa says. When it came to competitive games, Norris was a better pool player anyway—he was naturally analytical and an ace with the angles.

Long-time observers of William Norris say his Depression-era farm life had lasting impact. They talk about his fight for survival and daring innovations with common weeds for cattle feed. They suggest that Norris inherited the entrepreneurial instinct at least in part from his father and grandfather. They talk about Norris learning early to take risks and growing up with a social conscience born of Franklin Roosevelt's reforms and seeing his neighbors and family suffer hard times.

As much as he ached to leave it, Norris himself later recognized the value of prairie farm life. "You have meaningful things to do," he said recently, "and you're part of an enterprise. A successful farm embodies entrepreneurship. I had chances to work for money on many different jobs. We shared the rewards, and we shared the hardships. You learn to tinker and become an artist with baling wire. You don't have all the nuts, bolts and cables required to fix a piece of machinery, so you look around and make do. Farm life taught us to be ingenious. And, like any boy on the farm, I found out early who I was. I had a sense of identity."

Norris left the farm in 1934 to take a job with Westinghouse selling x-ray equipment. He was at first a reticent salesman, not given to the hard sell. "I wasn't putting enough pressure on at the right time," he says. "Like approaching a mule in the barn at home—I didn't slap the mule on the butt and say, 'Where's my order?' I was a little bit afraid of that mule...." Later on, with practice, however, Norris says he became "a hell of a good salesman."

Even before the United States entered World War II, Norris left Westinghouse and went to work as an electrical engineer for the Navy in Washington. When war was declared, he was commissioned in the Naval Reserve and assigned to Communications Supplementary Activity —CSAW, or "seesaw" for short, a "spook" outpost. The quickly assembled CSAW unit operated out of Mount Vernon Seminary, an erstwhile girls' school. Lieutenant Commander Norris and a select team of cryptologists, mathematicians, chess masters, bridge masters, physicists and engineers went to work breaking enemy codes. Norris designed systems for that code-breaking. "It was a massive undertaking," Norris says now. "First you had to get the transmission, then get information that offered some clues about how to proceed. Then you had to sort through massive amounts of data, collate it and work through it. Underneath it all lay a need to proceed even though you couldn't see all the answers."

While those activities were highly classified, observers of CSAW believe the seeds of the computer era were sown in those code-breaking exercises. Certainly, they say, manipulating masses of data was fundamental to code-breaking. And if a computer was to emerge, it would likely surface in a place like a CSAW lab. "The lore has it that Norris did something pretty remarkable to speed the code-breaking process," says Tom Kamp, a Control Data Corporation executive who has known Norris since 1957. "That era was personally influential. It helped him see once again that things could be done if he wanted to do them badly enough."

At the end of the war, a return to selling x-ray equipment for Westinghouse seemed all too prosaic for Norris. His CSAW colleague, Commander Howard Engstrom, a math professor at Yale, felt the same. Why not, Engstrom said, start a company and continue the work of CSAW? Code-breaking was just as important to national security in peacetime, he reasoned. Furthermore, the Navy would go out of its way to keep the CSAW brain power intact.

But it was not a good time to raise money for a new venture. In 1945, America's economic outlook was uncertain. There were no venture capital companies to court, and Wall Street investment bankers could see little promise in a firm that offered a service so highly classified that Norris and Engstrom couldn't even describe it. Give it up, they were told, and try television.

Then just before the CSAW brain trust scattered for civilian life, Norris and Engstrom found their angel in John E. Parker—investment banker, Annapolis graduate, a man well-connected in Washington political and military circles. Parker was a good businessman, an energetic salesman and a natural entrepreneur. He was no stranger to fledgling technology companies, either. His firm had invested in a light-plane manufacturer and later glider construction during the war. Parker would take another risk.

So it was that Engineering Research Associates, Inc. (ERA), was incorporated in St. Paul, Minnesota, in January 1946. Fifty percent of the company was owned by the founding fathers—Norris, Engstrom and a handful of other CSAW alumni—and 50 percent was owned by Parker and his investment group. Each group put up $10,000 (100,000 shares of ERA stock at 10 cents each). Parker also agreed to provide a $200,000 line of credit.

Unwilling to let this entrepreneurial effort blessed with top-secret contracts operate too independently, the U.S. government sent a polite "spy" (and CSAW veteran) to monitor ERA. New employees were told ERA worked for government and industry. If they wanted to know more, they were given any of several cover stories. In truth, ERA was designing and building electronic data-processing and storage devices—computers and computer parts. And before long, ERA computers were noted for their sophisticated engineering features, their careful design and their reliability. ERA engineers like Seymour Cray, Bill Keye and Frank Mullaney were just beginning to flex their creative muscles.

□ The little company in St. Paul was making a name for itself, but journalist Jack Anderson's "Washington Merry-Go-Round" column published in 1950 provided too much attention. Anderson and his colleague Tom McNamara complained that the Navy had entrusted a vital project "involving complex engineering and construction to an inexperienced company." Not only that, the newshounds pointed out, former Navy officers including William Norris and Howard Engstrom just happened to be "highly salaried" ERA vice presidents. A "juicy" multimillion-dollar contract had been awarded to ERA even though 12 established companies were available to do the work.

The enterprising little computer company that landed that "juicy" contract also attracted the attention of Remington Rand. James Rand had already purchased Eckert-Mauchly Computer Corporation, the developer of UNIVAC and ERA's arch-competitor. Like ERA, Eckert-Mauchly had suffered chronic cash shortages and finally succumbed to acquisition just before the start of the Korean War.

John Parker had begun thinking about selling out, too. ERA had been a good investment, he reasoned, but strictly a business deal. While ERA was growing, month-to-month financing was tough. Parker guessed that ERA needed at least $5 million, maybe $10 million, if it seriously hoped to enter the computer business in a major way.

Parker decided he would find a buyer for this promising but expensive enterprise. IBM, Honeywell and NCR were among the companies quietly examining ERA, but it was James Rand who finally bought ERA for 73,000 shares of Remington Rand common stock worth about $1.7 million on the New York Stock Exchange. Parker and Rand arrived at that sum by multiplying $5,000 times 340, the total number of engineers employed by ERA. "That may have been one of the few times since the Civil War," computer historians and engineers Arnold Cohen and Erwin Tomash observed later, "that individuals have been sold by the head outside the professional sports world."

When Parker announced the sale to ERA's shareholder-engineers in December 1951, they were shocked. Especially William Norris. The sale meant that Norris and his cadre of bright, young engineers would lose their creative freedom. They would be absorbed into massive Remington Rand, an entity about as fast on its feet as an aging government bureaucrat, an entity fiercely committed to the prosaic—electric shavers and typewriters. Equally important, the sale of ERA extinguished—at least for a while—an entrepreneurial flame. "Parker was a financier, and ERA was an investment," says Bill Drake. "The rest of us saw ERA as a commitment."

"Bill Norris thought John Parker sold us out," says Hank Forrest, an ERA engineer who's since been a Control Data senior vice president. "We could have sold shares in ERA...we could have made it work," Robert Perkins, another ERA engineer, says. "Bill Norris grumbled loud about it. He believed ERA could make it alone and beat everyone else out. We all saw potential, but Bill saw even more. Control Data became the second generation ERA."

"ERA would have changed the whole structure of the computer industry," Norris says today. "We had enormous technology, and we were much more advanced than any other company in important respects. If we'd had financing, we might have been the IBM of the industry. Had ERA *and* Eckert-Mauchly been able to continue independently, they both would have dominated the computer industry."

Even after the two computer firms were absorbed by Remington Rand, Norris is convinced, all they would have needed was a strong commitment from within the parent corporation to make it big. "But the people at Remington Rand just weren't willing to take the risk," Norris says, shaking his head, "so they lost a chance."

ERA and Eckert-Mauchly were tossed together in the same RemRand arena. There was jealousy between them and competition for corporate attention and appropriations. Each viewed the other as less than equal. Eckert-Mauchly engineers were the clever ones, innovative but also impractical. ERA may have seemed stodgy by comparison, but ERA hardware worked—and sold. ERA had become a major computer supplier to the Armed Forces. By 1954, insiders estimated that ERA had earned back its entire purchase price for RemRand.

ERA kept its outpost in St. Paul, and Eckert-Mauchly stayed in Philadelphia. Neither one wanted to move to RemRand's home base in Norwalk, Connecticut. (There was yet a third, internal computer group there.) Engineers at both outpost firms were independent thinkers, and observers believed Remington Rand chose to pit them against each other for the product gains "creative tension" might produce. Eckert-Mauchly built commercial computers led by UNIVAC 1. ERA built computers for scientific applications. Each team guarded its turf tenaciously.

As leader of the ERA team, Norris lived and worked with that tension. "RemRand in 1952 was not a unified company," historians Cohen and Tomash report; "it was an uncoordinated collection of fiefdoms...." Only tenuous links—financial, administrative and technical—existed among the various groups. The key ingredients of mutual respect and teamwork were absent. Both ERA and Eckert-Mauchly ignored the laboratories at Norwalk, and it was business as usual for the remainder of the RemRand organization, about 95 percent of the company, which remained totally uninvolved in electronic computers.

"With this uncoordinated business approach," Cohen and Tomash write, "RemRand soon started to lose ground." IBM was producing stiff competition in the marketplace and doing what William Norris wanted to do—capitalize on the commercial computer business and do it with aggressive marketing. Then, in 1955, RemRand merged with Sperry and consolidated its computer efforts, putting all the disparate factions under one man in a single St. Paul-based electronic computer division called UNIVAC. The man in charge was William Norris.

Sperry Rand, as it happened, provided a varied education for Bill Norris. Robert Price, current president of Control Data, says, "As Bill looks around now, he understands human foibles very well. He gained a perspective on the workings of a big corporation at Sperry Rand. He saw how a CEO could operate. Here was Sperry Rand, a company with a golden apple dropped in its lap. And what did it do? It manhandled the opportunity."

There was also General Douglas MacArthur, board chairman of Sperry Rand from 1955 to 1964. Norris admired MacArthur for his intellect, for his ideas and his ability to communicate. MacArthur turned up at Sperry Rand headquarters in Norwalk, Connecticut, on Thursdays. "He'd go up for lunch and then he'd sit around there and reminisce," Norris told a reporter. "Oh, boy, that was fantastic. I worked it out so I made my visit to Mecca on Thursdays, too. Invariably he would invite me to ride back in his car to New York."

During the nearly two-hour ride, Norris picked the general's brain. "There is no such thing as security in this world. There is only opportunity." Norris told the general he had made that axiom a part of his life when he heard it in a speech MacArthur delivered at commencement exercises in Nebraska.

"Well," MacArthur said, with a cynical smirk, "I can't remember it. But it sounds like something I would say."

□ The unification of Sperry Rand's computer groups under William Norris brought together research, engineering, manufacturing, marketing and finance. Now UNIVAC had great promise.

"The chief executive officer of Sperry said he wanted to be another IBM, he didn't want to be number two, and he had the resources to do it," Norris recalls. "I was a damn fool to believe him. It wasn't true, particularly the willingness.

"When Jim Rand bought Eckert-Mauchly and ERA, he thought he was getting products that he could immediately use to kick the hell out of IBM. But we didn't have products, we had knowledge leading up to products. When he found it was going to cost him hundreds of millions of dollars, he sold to Sperry. I don't think Sperry realized the risk and investment required."

Important appropriations were denied the UNIVAC division, and Norris' authority was steadily eroded. "The management of Sperry Rand turned on him and tore the division to pieces," says Robert Schmidt, an ERA veteran. "We were losing programs; we were losing capital appropriations," says Robert Perkins. "One by one, each of Norris' areas of jurisdiction was being pulled away," says Arnold Cohen, "...just like pulling feathers out of a pillow."

"Bill Norris was more an entrepreneur than an engineer," says Jim Thornton, founder of Network Systems in Minneapolis. "He intended to build a company. What really got him was reassignment of the entire marketing operation to someone else. He could see he was losing control of a situation he would lose further. It's not that he wasn't doing a good job. Sperry Rand just didn't know what they had."

"Bill finally became vice president of Sperry Rand," Bob Perkins says. "He was winning, but there was a lot of pressure for ambitious product development. In those days, we hadn't configured anything. When we did a job, we did it for the first time. If Bill could have seen a straight shot to the presidency in 1957, I believe he would have stayed. But entrepreneurs have trouble if they have to climb up through a heavy organizational structure. They don't all quit. Some adapt, and that's the end of their entrepreneurial spirit. Bill Norris chose *not* to adapt."

Some UNIVAC responsibilities were reassigned to old-line Rand people—the loyalists from shavers, punch cards and typewriters. The UNIVAC chain of command changed. James Rand turned Norris over to his son, Marcel. "He's an idiot," Norris snorts, "and I don't say that about people who don't qualify. It took me about three meetings with Marcel to figure out he didn't understand what I was talking about."

Strong words perhaps, but William Norris was a man seeing his enterprise dismantled. "They began to whack off this and whack off that, and finally they whacked off too much," Norris recalls. "I think accomplishment is the hallmark of an entrepreneur. If you can't accomplish something, you can't live. I was thwarted. It's nonsense that kills entrepreneurs, and I'd had enough nonsense at UNIVAC."

He was, in fact, ripe for a change when Arnold Ryden, a financial consultant, Byron Smith, a UNIVAC executive, and Willis Drake, Norris' assistant, approached him early in 1957.

"When Bill Norris steadily lost his responsibilities, there was no explanation except politics," Bill Drake says. "He was a strong guy, a confident guy. He had settled in to run the UNIVAC division in St. Paul believing Sperry Rand would finally see the light. St. Paul was the only profit center; the rest of UNIVAC was losing a lot of dough. Bill Norris was identified with making St. Paul the profit center. He was the kind people would rally around."

Against that backdrop, Drake says, Arnold Ryden began thinking out loud about a spin-off company—another ERA, perhaps, free to grow without corporate fetters. "What Arnold suggested was exciting but ethereal," says Drake. "Arnold knew how to build the business and financial plan. He knew how to give it shape so it might attract Bill Norris and others."

About the time that extracurricular project was taking shape, Drake says, things were going "from bad to impossible at UNIVAC. Morale plummeted to zero." Ryden and Byron Smith talked to Norris. Ryden talked to Frank Mullaney, then chief engineer of UNIVAC's military division. Ryden quietly talked to select others. "Ryden was the catalyst," according to Drake. "He distilled the idea of a new company on paper, and he had all the roles in mind.

It was to be a Bill Norris program."

"Bill Norris was older than the rest of us," says Mullaney. "We all worked for him. We assumed he would be the leader. He had the ability to get to the core of the problem. He had amazing persistence. He had marketing savvy, he knew how to go after government contracts. He had demonstrated the entrepreneurial spark early at ERA. I never felt that he was an amazing administrator, but he had all the other qualities the rest of us didn't.

"Bill and I met at the Criterion Restaurant in June 1957. 'I've had it,' he told me. 'I've tried to make it work through all the changes at UNIVAC and Sperry Rand. I know you've been talking to Arnold Ryden, too.' "

When Norris gave up on Sperry Rand and declared it, the exodus began. Bill Drake was first to leave. He was the new company's first employee, paid a modest salary with funds put up by Norris and Ryden. Drake had no nest egg. He had a family and house payments to make. He worked out of an office in the McGill Building in downtown Minneapolis, and his objective was to raise capital, "which we didn't have."

Sell stock, his collaborators said. It was an extraordinary idea. Never in history, the Minnesota securities commissioner told Drake, have the founders of a new company personally tried to sell their own stock.

Drake showed the commissioner the Control Data prospectus. (The company's name came from a collaborative effort at Norris' modest home in St. Paul, says Frank Mullaney. "We put down all the words that came to mind—data, electronic, computer. 'How about Control Data?' somebody said. 'What kind of a name is that?' I asked. It didn't mean anything to me, but, in the end, I was outvoted.") Control Data's mission statement was thin. The company would engage in research and development of electronic equipment. Nothing was said about building computers. Furthermore, the company said it did not intend to compete directly with giants like IBM, Sperry Rand and General Electric.

The securities commissioner searched his rule books looking for some regulation that outlawed personal sale of new company stock by its founders. There was none. He handed Drake all the forms he needed and expected never to see him again.

"The idea that we could sell stock in a company with no product, no employees and no facility seemed totally preposterous to him," Drake recalls. Drake set about trying to sell the stock anyway. He drank countless cups of coffee at Mrs. Strandy's Coffee Shop in St. Paul with potential investors. He met others at the Parker House Restaurant in Mendota ("when people didn't want to be seen with me"). But the process was too slow. Drake invited a dozen people to his home instead.

"One engineer said he wanted 10,000 shares," Drake recalls. "Up to that time I had sold 500. The second night we had another meeting; this time 25 people showed up. The third night, there were cars parked for blocks up and down the street in every direction. People called from New York and California. The whole thing cascaded. Investors were buying the principals led by William Norris as much as they were buying the idea for a company."

One objective was to distribute Control Data stock as widely as possible. The future of this new venture, the cofounder decided, would not be vested in a single large shareholder like John Parker.

The stock sold easily—615,000 shares at $1 a share in less than two weeks. About 300 people, chiefly UNIVAC employees and personal friends of Control Data officers, invested. Norris himself bought 75,000 shares—having "mortgaged nearly everything to do that," according to a colleague. Then Norris and Ryden arranged a two-year note with First Bank of Minneapolis for the principal investors. The bank was willing to lend each man four times his investment, with his Control Data stock pledged as collateral. ("That," Bill Drake says, "was an enlightened bank.") Even Jane Norris, Bill Norris' wife, put in some of her own money for Control Data stock. "If we lose all of it," she said at the time, "we'll just move ourselves and our six children back to the farm in Nebraska."

Norris was quick, however, to advise his friends that Control Data was a high-risk investment. Don't come crying to me, he'd say, if we're a wash-out. Even so, they were fascinated. Norris' roommate from his Westinghouse days, Dr. Archie Barrett, was eager to buy. "But he said he had trouble visualizing what I was talking about," Norris says. Norris had been gone about six weeks from UNIVAC at the time. He decided to return with Barrett to show him a UNIVAC machine firsthand.

"My God, is this what you're talking about?" Barrett asked.

"Well, yeah," Norris answered. "You realize it's a long step between where we are and that piece of machine."

"Oh, yeah, yeah," Barrett said. "I understand that, but I'm in." Barrett became a major shareholder. Though the mission statement suggested otherwise, Bill Norris was thinking big.

Soon there were more buyers than there were Control Data shares available, and the exodus from UNIVAC began in earnest. "Bill Norris was the key guy to go," Jim Thornton recalls. "By the time Control Data stock was issued in September, we also knew Frank Mullaney would leave. He tipped the balance for our engineers. There was a lot of speculation about who would leave to join CDC."

After Norris and Mullaney left, Jim Miles, Bill Keye, Bob Perkins, Hank Forrest, Seymour Cray and others in third and fourth waves followed after them. Those who abandoned UNIVAC in search of new high-tech worlds —some 50 of them—were dubbed the "Mayflower crew."

"It seemed like several times a week we had a farewell lunch for somebody," Arnold Cohen recalls. "The next guy who resigns to join Control Data," a UNIVAC colleague declared, "can buy his own damn lunch!"

The farewells began in September 1957 and continued for almost a year. "We heard that Sperry Rand hired a private investigator to copy the license numbers of cars parked in front of Bill Norris' home during that period," Cohen says. "The management didn't know what was going on at first," says Hank Forrest. "Later on, they saw the exodus, and their attitude turned to paranoia."

The next event was foreshadowed:

Norris visited the aging elder statesman of Minnesota Mining & Manufacturing, William McKnight. Norris painted vivid pictures of Control Data and asked for McKnight's involvement. "Hell," the 70-year-old 3M chairman said, "if I were 20 years younger, I'd invest. And I'll tell you this, too, sonny: If I were Remington Rand UNIVAC, I'd sue your ass."

It did, in fact. Sperry Rand's lawsuit alleged that Norris and other UNIVAC alumni walked off with trade secrets. "Their charges were absolutely ridiculous," Mullaney insists. "They accused us of taking classified material. We didn't; we didn't even know what we were going to do. The suit dragged on a couple years, and then it was settled without a dollar exchanged."

The Control Data co-founders did sign a consent order promising they would not use certain information they might have gleaned from their UNIVAC days. "We agreed we wouldn't do this, we agreed we wouldn't do that," Mullaney says. "They were things we wouldn't do anyway." Notoriety surrounding the lawsuit didn't hurt. It drew valuable public attention to the young company. A year after Sperry Rand filed suit, the per-share value of Control Data stock rose from 33 cents to $11.25.

☐ Almost everyone but William Norris remembers the early years of Control Data as a collaborative effort. Norris and Ryden were busy raising capital and drafting bids for government contracts. Mullaney and Cray were hard at work on designs. Others made sales calls and handled small contract assignments that filtered in. "It started as a collaborative effort," says Arnold Ryden. "We even took pay cuts or sacrificed pay checks to stay on."

"When an enterprise begins—that's a beautiful period," says Bill Drake. "You have clear, shared objectives. There's so much to do that no one can work hard enough or long enough to get it all done."

"You don't get people into a little boat on a collaborative effort," Norris argues, however. "Sure, they wanted to jump in the boat, but they knew damn well who was running it. There was never an idea of a communal effort...not even in the beginning." Of other opinions to the contrary he says: "That's a great compliment to me...that they would feel they were running the ship."

There was at least one shared objective among the Control Data class of '57, and that involved the size of the company. "Initially, the emphasis was on keeping Control Data small," says Hank Forrest. "Every guy that left Sperry Rand was obsessed with the strictures of a big corporation." Norris agrees: "There was never any plan to get big. There was always a nostalgia around Control Data—it would be nice not to get large."

Nostalgia aside, Norris could see the advantage of size and the importance of growth for competition's sake. He conceded one day, after Control Data's first two acquisitions aimed at expanding its business, "I suppose we're going to be a big company some day."

Indeed, Norris embarked on a series of early acquisitions aimed at building what he called "critical mass." In December 1957, just four months after Control Data's founding, the firm acquired Cedar Engineering Company, a manufacturer of electronic instruments and control devices. "Cedar nearly busted us," Norris once told a reporter. "It took about $500,000 in cash to turn it around. We cut everybody's salary in half to conserve cash."

But Control Data needed Cedar Engineering. Before the acquisition, CDC had no more than a small design and assembly operation to show potential investors, customers and tax accountants. Cedar offered a physical plant and manufacturing capability. Not long after that purchase, Control Data acquired Control Corporation of Minneapolis—and there would be many more. "Norris got his critical mass," says Frank Mullaney. "It didn't matter so much that all those entities would be profitable. In those days, if a company was failing, the word was, 'Pass it by Bill Norris...he'll buy it.' A lot of Control Data stock went for those acquisitions. We called the stock we bought them with 'Chinese money.' "

For the most part, William Norris says, that acquisitive period added new technology, staff and physical plant to the fledgling Control Data. There were "dogs" in the lot, he admits, "but we hustled them out." He says he had to play the percentages in building Control Data's critical mass. "We acquired one company called CEIR for 267,404 shares of stock, and it never made any money. But we got people and technology. And one of the most profitable entities we have today came from that dog—our Arbitron service."

"It became clear that Bill Norris' idea was to build Control Data quickly," says Jim Thornton. "Get the revenue growth up early, recognizing that profitability won't be there. The acquisitive style suited him. Bill has always been one to juggle and see which venture emerges as a good one."

"He has a way of turning losers into winners," says Bill Keye. " 'Big companies aren't smarter than small ones,' he would say, 'but they have enough resources to stay with an idea, capitalize it and wait out the success.' "

Norris doggedly hung on to those ventures he knew had validity, unprofitable or not. Criticism, within and outside of Control Data, did not sway him. "I've always told people around here," he says, "that garnering criticism is better than being ignored. One of the things I learned from UNIVAC was the utter wastefulness of starting things and turning them off because earnings might go down. When we hit adversity, we slow down our effort, but we never cancel a project that still makes sense." In the early days of Control Data, Norris was even blunter on the subject: "There ain't no backin' up," he would say.

Bill Norris distinguished himself early as a tireless worker and creature of habit. He routinely logged 12- and 14-hour days and carried briefcases home loaded with work. "Bill Norris is a workoholic," says Hank Forrest. "He has always had a sense of urgency." "Norris' lunches were the same day after day," says Tom Kamp. "A hamburger and a Coke, 11:45 a.m., at the same Howard Johnson's restaurant." Pleasure was always secondary to the task. Norris was the entrepreneurial ascetic.

Under Norris' direction, the young company saved money in every way it could. When Hank Forrest's phone bill was $53 in the first two months of business, Norris prohibited long-distance calls and insisted Forrest handle all communications in writing. Control Data staffers always told a manufacturer's representative selling electronic parts to arrive at 11:30 a.m., hoping he would buy them lunch. "I don't mind feeding the company," the rep said one day when he was asked to leave yet another armload of parts behind, "but I'll be damned if you're going to build your computer with my samples."

That computer was Seymour Cray's 1604—an instrument that would set Control Data's course for years to come and pull it out of its early poverty. Cray's 1604 meant that Control Data would not be the company described in the original mission statement. CDC would instead build a large-scale computer, and it would compete with the majors. The 1604 was compact, extremely versatile and, most important, priced at about half the cost of a competitive IBM computer. The 1604 was predicated on transistors, not vacuum tubes, and designed with complex printed circuit cards. "Printed building blocks," Cray called the cards. With those as a starting point, he theorized, a computer of almost any size could be built.

"No one else at Control Data would have thought of it," says Robert Kisch, a CDC engineer during that period. "No one else had the capability. The initial success of Control Data was due to Seymour Cray."

The 1604 had its debut eight months after Control Data was incorporated. Two months later the company had its first order from the U.S. Navy Bureau of Ships. The $1.5-million sale to a "prestige customer" was crucial to the young company's credibility. About the same time, Norris, the man responsible for fund-raising, had also convinced Allstate Insurance to buy 350,000 shares of preferred stock at $25 per share. "We were rolling again on a full stomach," Norris recalls.

After the Navy order, new buyers of the 1604 fell into line, and Cray continued his imaginative tinkering. In 1959, Cray's Model 160 desk-sized computer selling for $90,000 enhanced the company's growing reputation for innovation. A year after that, Cray started work on the CDC 6600—bigger than IBM's "Stretch," until that time the largest computer ever built. The 6600 would cost $7 million per unit, and Norris offered a reporter the following understatement: "We won't have to make very many to make money...."

When Norris said in 1961, with similar understatement, "There are certain advantages to size," perhaps even he did not envision the momentum of that decade. After its first, unprofitable year, when total sales hovered around $780,000, CDC's figures were stunning: 1959, $4.5 million; 1960, $28 million; 1963, $100 million; 1965, $160 million; 1968, $841 million; 1969, $1 billion.

In 1961, only IBM, with a hammerlock on 82 percent of the computer market, and Control Data, with 1.6 percent of the market, were operating in the black. The computer divisions of Philco, Bendix, RCA, Packard-Bell and Honeywell all saw red ink. Norris' nemesis, Sperry Rand, was only just approaching profitability with its computers.

In those go-go years of the '60s, Control Data sold computers to such diverse customers as the U.S. Department of Commerce, the University of Montreal, the government of Switzerland, NASA (for the Apollo moon flight) and Bell

Laboratories. By 1963, Control Data had expanded into overseas markets, with subsidiaries in Australia, the Netherlands, Sweden, Switzerland, West Germany and France. By 1967, CDC was operating in 20 countries.

Norris' acquisitive strategy, meanwhile, continued apace—six acquisitions in 1964, nine more in 1965, 10 more in 1967. Those acquisitions strengthened Control Data's hand in the computer-peripherals business, the data-services business, the software business, even the loan business with purchase of Commercial Credit for approximately $745 million in CDC stock. The ventures into new fields were not all popular decisions, but Norris cared little about popularity. "Whenever I see everybody going south," he declared years later, "I have a great compulsion to go north."

□ Thomas Watson Jr., IBM's chairman of the board, was piqued by the David-and-Goliath comparisons between his company and the upstart CDC in Minneapolis. "I fail to understand," he complained to his board, "why we have lost our industry leadership position by letting someone else offer the world's most powerful computer."

Why indeed? Watson and IBM would not sit still for it. IBM responded with a double whammy—"fighting machines," modified electronic equipment with much lower pricetags, and "paper machines," computers that never go beyond the design stage.

The effect was devastating. Early in 1961, when Seymour Cray's 1604 was garnering market attention, IBM took its Model 7090, made modifications and sold it at a much lower price to compete with the 1604. For almost a year, Norris says, Control Data was unable to land a single order for a 1604. Cray got busy adding new features to the 1604, and Control Data answered the challenge later in 1961 with a 1604-A.

IBM retaliated with a 7094, an upgraded 7090.

Control Data answered with a more powerful 3600.

IBM volleyed with a 7094 II.

The battle of the bytes, the real and imagined computers, continued until December 1968, when David finally challenged Goliath in the courtroom.

"IBM was more than formidable—they were killing us in the marketplace," Bob Kisch recalls. "Bill Norris was furious," says Hank Forrest. " 'Somebody's got to do something!' he howled. The other alternative was to lay back and try to weather the storm. I was against the suit. It was a terrible strain on our management and development staff. I said that a couple of times...and shut up."

Forrest was not alone in his opposition. The corporate counsel was wary of an expensive, protracted and perhaps "unwinnable" lawsuit, but Norris was adamant. "When he's determined to do something, nothing gets in his way," says Bob Kisch. "Bill Norris has a tenacity of a bulldog."

"If we lost, we could have lost the whole company," says Tom Kamp. "Bill went around the room and asked everyone their opinion. We each got a chance to say what we wanted. In typical Bill Norris fashion, he had made up his mind. He knew what he wanted to do."

"On two occasions, they damn near put us out of business, and I felt I would be remiss if I allowed it to happen again," Norris explains today. "I began to collect evidence after the first time. The second time convinced me there wouldn't be a third. You have to do what you have to do." Norris is still convinced he was battling for the very survival of Control Data. To "lay back and try to weather the storm," Norris believes, was no alternative at all. That simply meant, he says, "making a decision about where you want to die."

"We met and met, we talked and talked," says Norris. "Finally I said, 'This is what we're going to do.' Some people shook their heads, some nodded affirmative. One of our directors told me IBM would kick the hell out of us. He denies that now, but I wrote it down." ("Norris usually took minutes at management committee meetings," Bob Kisch recalls. "When they were printed, they always reflected how William Norris thought things were discussed....")

While taking on IBM, Norris also looked for other market possibilities. "We kept building big computers," says Bob Price, "but Bill also looked for other things we could do. Bill Norris has a will to survive. He didn't bloody his head. At the time he was fighting the battle with IBM, he was searching for new niches."

One niche was IBM's Service Bureau Corporation, ceded to Control Data as part of the final IBM-CDC settlement in 1973. When IBM chairman Vin Learson chose to do the unthinkable and discuss a settlement alone with Norris in an Omaha hotel room, SBC was what Norris wanted. SBC had been a leader in time-sharing and data services, and Norris now says it was worth far more than it appeared in 1973.

Norris was actively involved in the IBM litigation. He says he spent "hours and hours" studying the case and the Sherman and Clayton antitrust acts. He criticized other firms with antitrust suits against IBM for leaving the responsibility to "inept lawyers." Control Data's suit against IBM escalated into one of the largest and most complex antitrust actions in history. Eventually, executives of three other computer manufacturers—Sperry Rand, Honeywell and NCR—joined CDC in asking the Justice Department to put limits on IBM's competitive activities.

The CDC-IBM case was finally settled out of court in 1973. Control Data received tangible and intangible benefits worth an estimated $100 million, plus SBC. In addition, the computer program CDC developed to index, summarize, sort and retrieve mountains of information connected with the long, complicated legal action became a marketable legal service that Control Data could offer to other companies.

Ironically, it was Norris' penchant for pursuing new markets and expanding the Control Data product line that finally drove out purists like Seymour Cray and Frank Mullaney. Norris had moved into producing peripheral products—memories, printers, disk drives, tape drives, all the paraphernalia that allows a large, mainframe computer to do its job. What's more, CDC was selling its peripherals to the competition. Norris had also moved into data services—sharing computer power among customers who can't afford their own computers and, later, developing tailored "software" programs to suit specific needs. In the opinion of some, Norris was "betting the company every two to three years." To people like Cray and Mullaney, Control Data was diverting its capital from computers to services and peripherals. The company was getting too large for their sensibilities.

☐ If there *was* a spirit of collaboration among Control Data's founders, it ended in the late 1960s. "Seymour Cray was designing machines we didn't build," says Bob

Perkins. "He said, 'Hell, I'll quit and start a business of my own.' His start-up capital came from CDC cronies."

"I remember Frank Mullaney saying that if Bill Norris had taken an afternoon off to visit Seymour's lab in Chippewa Falls, Seymour might have been willing to stay. But Cray was restless, and he didn't feel he had the attention he needed," says Arnold Cohen. "It's a challenge managing millionaires [by this time, the co-founders who bought $1 stock were worth at least a million]. If they choose to go off on their own, they can."

"Cray and I wanted a hardware company, Bill Norris wanted a service company. That's where the parting occurred," says Frank Mullaney, who later invested big in Cray Research. "Bill had more chips. He was running the company. The direction Control Data took was mainly Bill's choice. There wasn't much point in thinking we could do it any other way."

"Control Data was the greatest act of collaboration I've seen," says Bill Drake, who left Control Data and co-founded Data Card, "then Bill took back the helm. The 'we're-all-equal' idea no longer worked. A hierarchy develops as a company grows, and decisions have to be made. Somebody finally survives."

Will Rogers' observation may have applied to Norris and some of the co-founders who eventually fell away from Control Data: "A difference of opinion is what makes horse racing—and missionaries," Rogers said. Certainly their differences finally divided the co-founders, but Bill Norris and his entrepreneurial style may have spawned more of the former than the latter. Seymour Cray left CDC to start Cray Research in the quiet woods of Wisconsin with Frank Mullaney, a major investor. Jim Thornton founded Network Systems, and Bill Drake co-founded Data Card. Arnold Ryden became an independent consultant again. Jim Miles became a venture capitalist.

Bill Norris seemed genuinely sorry to see his compatriots go, but he wished them well. He says he left the door open to them and invested in some of their ventures. But he never looked back. "I've seen several people think they couldn't be replaced around Control Data," says Tom Kamp, "and they have been." The only exception perhaps is Norris himself.

True, he has established an "executive office" and given

more responsibility to his "co-heirs," Norbert Berg and Robert Price. True, Norris, at 71, does not concern himself so much with daily operations as he once did. But Norris is still very much a presence in the 14-story corporate headquarters in suburban Bloomington. He arrives there about 8:30 a.m. and works until about 4 p.m., when his driver takes him and his two briefcases packed with work to an earth-sheltered home in a Twin Cities suburb. The driver was a reluctant concession to Norris' status. At least, when he doesn't drive, Norris can pull down the folding table in the backseat and work en route.

"Bill is living at the center of his newest newfangled dreams," says Frank Mullaney. In his later years, Norris has gone from computer engineer to social engineer, committing Control Data and its resources to ventures that both serve society and, he expects, turn a profit. Projects include: revitalization of urban neighborhoods, the survival of the small farm, alternative energy sources, individualized learning programs for students of all ages, encouragement of fledgling entrepreneurs and their new ventures. The connective tissue binding these projects together is the computer.

Critics who point out that Rural Venture, City Venture and PLATO (Computer-Based Education) programs have yet to turn a profit call these newfangled dreams the "good works department" of Control Data. But Bill Norris scoffs at what he considers their shortsighted judgment and marches on to the next project.

"He has a high opinion of his opinion," says Mullaney, "and that's what an entrepreneur has to have. Certainly, Bill Norris has to have foresight, but guts—that's what he has the most of."

"William Norris has great self-confidence," Tom Kamp says. "If it's a good idea he's undeterred by logical persuasion or discussion. I've never seen him doubt his own judgment. And nobody threatens Bill Norris. I don't care who you are, IBM or the president of the United States. He's tough-fibered, and he's persistent. When he makes a decision, he plows ahead."

Bill Norris, it is said, has an enormous grasp of basic human nature, he is a shrewd salesman, he has incredible self-discipline, he can see farther than most people, he can focus. He has almost no tolerance for mistakes, he is egotistical, he is demanding, he is cold, he is blunt, he is a loner, he is a peasant visionary. He is a man who inspires ready description.

When he assesses himself, he says his greatest strength is his willingness to take risks. "That's fundamental to the entrepreneurial life," he says. "You have to thrive on risk-taking. It comes with practice...and the process. That doesn't mean you get careless, but you do acquire new talents. Ten years ago, I wouldn't have considered an undertaking like Rural Venture...or PLATO. Today I do."

Norris believes his greatest weakness is hanging on to people too long, just as he has sometimes hung on to projects too long. "We have people who aren't making it around Control Data," he says. "The consensus is they should get another job or be let go. But I don't like to give up on people, or projects."

When he doubts, Norris says, he doubts the viability of America's economic system. "I'm trying to influence that system, but I'm not sure I can," he says. "When I confront doubt, it centers on achieving things beyond this company...beyond a sphere I have some control over."

Norris believes the survival instinct is crucial to the entrepreneur. "If something goes wrong, you reassess," he says. "There's nothing wrong with admitting a mistake, but don't stop, don't back up." And that may be the fundamental reason Bill Norris is still cradling Control Data's tiller.

There is a large mahogany ship's wheel in the anteroom of Norris' office at Control Data headquarters. The wheel is inscribed: "To our Helmsman from his crew—on settlement of the IBM lawsuit, January 1973.

"He chose a course that had no charter," the inscription reads. "He steered the ship and brought us through."

Perhaps William Norris was right all along about the small boat of "collaborators" set adrift back in 1957.

Richard Schaak

7

Richard Schaak

The Battler

At the age of 19, Richard Schaak had all the direction of a whirling dervish. He could run rings around the other members of his track team and execute the fanciest maneuvers with his uniformed drill squad at the College of St. Thomas, but he was no heavyweight in the classroom. He quit college in his second year. And while he had a knack for circuitry, he claimed he "couldn't stand electronics" and left the Northwestern School of Electronics 11 weeks before graduation.

Dick Schaak ambled across Minnehaha Avenue in south Minneapolis that same day to his father's struggling radio- and television-repair shop. Leander Schaak had started the small business less than two years earlier, in 1957, after spending nearly three decades working for others. Leander had had enough of common employment. He wanted to run his own show during the prosperous 1950s when consumer buying bloomed after wartime sacrifice.

"How about it, Dad?" Dick Schaak said to his earnest, Germanic father. "Let me work part-time here at the store before college starts again. I think they'll let me back in."

Leander Schaak eyed the dervish. The two weren't close—never were. Leander was not one to show emotion or outright interest in his son's activities. He had work to do. Dick didn't even know his father had slipped out of the store from time to time to take in his track meets at St. Thomas.

"All right, Dick," Leander nodded. "There's more here than I can do."

Eight weeks later, Leander Schaak died of cancer. The dervish was left to mind the store.

Richard and his mother Genevieve closed the shop Friday afternoon and appeared in their attorney's office Monday morning. The net worth of Schaak Electronics was $7,500. "We can sell for $5,000," Schaak said. "Some offer," he scoffed. "But if we sell now, Mother has at least $5,000. If she tried to run it herself, she might have to sell later, maybe at a lower price." Take a couple days to consider it, the attorney suggested, and we'll talk further.

Schaak considered the possibilities. "If you'll agree," Schaak finally told his mother, "I'll try to run the business. I don't know a thing about payables and receivables. I don't even enjoy electronics like Dad did, but I can sell." Genevieve Schaak agreed.

Richard Schaak crawled before he walked and walked some distance before he ran. He almost became a dropout again—this time to business bankruptcy. But this time Schaak stayed the course. And today's Schaak Electronics includes 49 electronics stores and eight Digital Dens serving up home computers and other high-tech gear in 15 cities throughout the Upper Midwest. Annual sales for fiscal 1982 will exceed $50 million. The dervish, it turned out, had both staying power and direction.

☐ Young Dick Schaak was a high achiever and a scrappy, street-smart runt. At 110 pounds in high school, he once took on a 180-pound adversary. "We got into a fight," Schaak recalls. "He beat me down to the ground. I went after him. Down again. Up again. After him. The kids finally broke it up. The guy was two years older, and that made a big difference. But I waited for him after school...and got beat up again. Even today, I'd like one more crack at him."

"I saw Richard occasionally," says Ray Ripley, a sales

representative and friend of the Schaak family. "He'd come into his father's store with one black eye or a puffed-up lip. He was a rough kid in school. He had a chip on his shoulder and somebody removed it frequently, including his father. Richard was a rebel. He wanted to tie the world into a knot. He didn't know how, but he was loaded with ambition."

Dick was smaller than most boys who went out for track or swimming at St. Thomas Academy. "I decided I had to work harder and set records," he says. "I was smaller so I had to exercise more. I wasn't a natural athlete so I worked hard to compensate." The runt set state records in swimming and track. He became the captain of both teams. "It wasn't that I had to be the best," he insists. "I just kept wondering, 'How good can I be?'"

Schaak also wanted to make the high school baseball team, but he had no glove. There was no way to get one, either. The folks couldn't afford one, and he couldn't scrape up the cash. "So the folks said, 'If you make the team you can get a glove.' I started playing third base without a glove and didn't think twice about it. I was determined to make it. They'd throw me a ball, and I'd catch it barehanded. But I also dropped it a lot...I just couldn't catch that well without a glove. I didn't make the team."

Schaak decided he was not that keen on team sports anyway. "It wasn't a good feeling, losing or winning with the whole team, based on what somebody else did," he says. "In an event like track, I knew I was a definite winner or a definite loser. On my own."

Schaak then took to making his own archery equipment, although his aim was faulty and he had little hope of achievement in that solitary sport. But if he couldn't hit the broad side of a barn, he reasoned, he'd at least sell his strings and arrows to those who could. So at 13, he peddled his homemade bowstrings and arrows at the Minnesota State Fair and hopped a bus to work the outstate tournaments. Schaak was pragmatic: "When you go to a tournament and competitors are involved in a field shoot, that means they're shooting into the woods, not at targets. They can lose a lot of arrows that way. I figured Dick Schaak's arrows and bow strings might not be quite as good as those sold down in the cities, but when you're at a shoot in Grand Rapids and Dick Schaak has the only concession, you buy Dick Schaak's goods.''

Schaak was an able salesman, but not exactly a numbers man: "I added up my cost of making arrows and bow strings, then added a buck to cover my bus ride. If I'd relied on that mark-up for profit, it would have been my first bankruptcy. At 13.''

Schaak was a daydreamer in school, but he was capable of surprising inquiry if it involved his own idea. When the six-year-old Schaak had an appendectomy, the first thing he did upon returning home was conduct the same operation on his stuffed bear. He painstakingly cut open the bear's side, extracted the "diseased" stuffing and sewed up the neat incision. He would carry that capacity for observation and self-study into adulthood.

In addition, the young Dick Schaak had faith in a force outside himself, and expected a great deal, his mother recalls. "If he woke up in the morning and couldn't find his socks, he knelt down and prayed to St. Anthony, the finder of lost things," she says. "He never thought to look under the bed. Dick always expected his prayers to be answered." Once, when he was ill with a sore throat and high temperature, he insisted that his parents bundle him up and take him to the neighborhood Catholic church for Candlemass Day. "He wanted," Genevieve Schaak says, "his throat blessed."

Early on, Dick Schaak learned about tithing from his exposure to Catholicism and Catholic schools. He started giving $1 a month in grade school to Maryknoll mission work. "The children were able to contribute toward the support of starving pagan children, as they were called then," says Genevieve Schaak. "He gave every month until he graduated from high school." And if some 180-pound lout called Schaak "goody two-shoes," the lout knew what to expect after school.

Dick Schaak took over the management of his father's store in 1960 with the same tenacity he'd shown as a boy. Schaak's store, 1,500 square feet at 39th Street and Minnehaha Avenue in south Minneapolis, was packed with transistors, vacuum tubes, batteries, radios and televisions. It was a "hole in the wall," by one customer's description—and receivables trailed far behind accounts paid in full. Even a 21-year-old novice could spot that.

"We had $12,000 owed us," Schaak recalls, "and

$1,500 in the checking account. The place to go was receivables to get the cash we needed to keep the business running. I started asking those guys to pay, and they said, 'Your father would never do that.' They were right, he wouldn't. Dad's old customers got mad and wouldn't buy from me. That's when I started advertising in the newspaper.''

Schaak was still an innocent, however, when he sat down at his father's old desk in the store's back room. "I didn't know anything about business," he says. "I'd never sold a radio. I leafed through Dad's invoices and didn't understand any of the terms—who's an FOB? I stayed up nights going through those invoices trying to figure out what every line meant. Then I'd open up the store at 8 a.m., close at 9 p.m., hit the sack and do the same all-nighter the following day. I had to work straight through to find out what the business was all about. I did it alone because I didn't know who to go to for help. Even if I had, I didn't know enough to ask even the most fundamental business questions.''

"When he walked into that store alone the first day, he walked in feeling blind," Pat Schaak, his wife, recalls. "He knew he could run the business, but he didn't know how. He believed it was all learnable. So he taught himself.''

With Schaak's venture into classified and, later, display newspaper ads, the store began to shift its emphasis from that of a parts distributor and repair shop to an audio house. Schaak began stocking hi-fi kits and speakers, turntables and tape recorders, diamond needles and intercoms. His customers began buying the big-ticket items, and they weren't just repairmen and ham radio enthusiasts. They were young people coming out of electronics trade schools, they were home hi-fi hobbyists and do-it-yourselfers. Schaak was no "electronic junk dealer," either—he was not buying distressed goods from manufacturers and re-selling them without a word of caution to naive customers. He was becoming instead an audio specialist. Soon he began seeing the business prosper in a way it had never prospered under his father. Dick Schaak was hot stuff.

"It was about six weeks before I realized that one thing Dad always did was take lunch with an electronics sales-man," he says. "They'd come in and he'd go out. Here it was six weeks and I hadn't seen a salesman or had a lunch out yet. Finally, my father's friend Ray Ripley called and asked if I had time.''

Before Schaak even had his topcoat off at the local greasy spoon, Ripley unloaded. "The only reason I'm here," he growled, "is because my wife said I owed it to your mother to come and talk to you. As far as I'm concerned, you're nothing but a hotheaded young punk. If we have an understanding, we can sit down and eat.''

"I took my coat off," Schaak says, "and for the first time in my life, I listened hard. I listened for two-and-a-half hours.''

"You may be on your way to success," Ripley said, "but, buddy, you have to learn how to treat people like human beings, including salesmen. They're your life's blood, and without them you're out of business.''

After lunch, Schaak says, he headed for Genevieve Schaak's basement to retrieve Leander's dog-eared copy of *How To Win Friends and Influence People*. "I'd gone through four years of high school and some college," Schaak says now, "and that was the first book I'd ever read all the way through." To a pragmatist like Schaak, it may well have been the first book he believed he could use. Since then Dick Schaak has read shelves full of books, from Peter Drucker to the Bible.

☐ From that single retail store in 1960, Schaak had expanded to 10 stores—eight in the Twin Cities, one in Rochester and one in St. Cloud—by 1971. He followed the Dayton Hudson Corporation into its highly successful covered shopping centers in the Twin Cities suburbs. He galloped past his father's dream of one, perhaps two, additional retail outlets. While Leander had hoped to make a steady, decent living, Richard planned to be the biggest and most prosperous operator in his industry. From 1,500 square feet of retail space in 1960, Schaak had expanded the business to about 40,000 square feet by 1972. From $140,000 in total sales, the figure had grown to $4.2 million. From five employees in 1960, Schaak's work force had increased to about 90 in 1972.

Schaak had little local competition at that point. The Team Electronics, Radio Shacks and Audio Kings of Minnesota would emerge later with an eye on carving up pieces of the market Schaak had developed. Only the industry old-timer, Allied, based in Chicago, gave Schaak pause.

Schaak, a millionaire at 33, became a "double millionaire" at 34 when Schaak Electronics' volume rose to $9 million in 1973. He had expanded into Chicago and Milwaukee and had his ambitious eyes trained on Denver and Atlanta. To finance his national expansion, he had taken his company public in September 1971, although he retained almost 80 percent of the ownership for himself. The stock had increased in value from $6 a share in September 1971 to $17 a share in June 1972. And even when financial disaster struck later, Schaak resolved to keep a majority of the stock. He would not "sell the store" out from under the Schaak family. Nor could he stand to relinquish personal control.

Schaak worked an average of 12 hours daily including some weekends. Pat Schaak and their three children saw virtually nothing of him. When he was home, he devoured industry journals and books on management theory. Schaak was a classic "seat of the pants" entrepreneur by his own definition—"doing everything, from signing checks to making deals to vacuuming the carpet." His work expanded to fill all the time available. It seemed necessary to justify his expanding bank account.

"Things were going great," he remembers. "I was making more money than I thought I would make in a lifetime." Still, he told Jack Klein, a long-time friend, one evening after closing the store, "I don't feel right. I'm just not happy. I'm in a successful business...but I don't know why I'm doing so well. I don't even know if I deserve it."

The string of 12-hour days helped Schaak feel more deserving. It also sent a message to his employees: If the boss was willing to pitch in with that level of enthusiasm, they had better keep pace. Particularly salespeople. Schaak was convinced that his company's success could be attributed, in large part, to employees who understood every item they sold. "We give all our employees a test every other week to see if they know the products we handle," Schaak told a reporter in 1972. "If they fail two consecutive tests, we let them go."

"He could be tough on employees," Jack Klein recalls. "He could fire a person very pointedly if things went wrong. If Dick took a great salesman and promoted him to vice president and then the man couldn't handle the new responsibilty, Dick believed the promotion could be reversed."

Dick Schaak was both a cheerleader and consummate energy source. His "fuel" was a relentless need to achieve. With his good looks and zeal, he was reminiscent of Jack Armstrong, all-American boy. "Morale," Schaak's employee newsletter intoned, "is faith in the man at the top." "When you start out in business," Schaak says now, "you absolutely have to believe that you are the root of success. You need a strong ego."

"Anyone who could work for that outfit for more than 15 minutes without being infected with lasting enthusiasm," a guest at Schaak's One and Only, Genuine Original Christmas Party held on the first day of spring 1973, said, "is in the wrong job."

Schaak's college buddy and vice president, Paul Ginther, further articulated the Schaak manifesto: "The man who does only as much work as he has to turns his job into a prison."

Dick Schaak would discover later that the analogy had bitter irony. For the moment, however, hard work and lots of it was the norm. Schaak was building an empire on his father's modest entry into the world of entrepreneurship. His decision in 1973 to more than double the size of Schaak Electronics with a single acquisition made that abundantly clear.

Allied Radio was no stranger to Schaak. During his first year in business, the kid hopped a train to Chicago to make a purchase at an Allied outlet on North Western Avenue. Schaak wanted to study his competition firsthand. At one point, that store alone produced $8.5 million in annual sales. When Schaak saw the chance to buy 27 Allied stores, including eight in Chicago, at a discount price ($340,000) he grabbed it. The Tandy Corporation had been forced to divest itself of Allied. Tandy was also the parent company of Radio Shack.

But Allied in 1973 was not the Allied of years earlier when the successful chain sold $90 million in radio and hi-fi gear. Minimal marketing efforts and tough competition had eroded Allied's solid position. By 1973, Allied's sales at 36 stores in the Upper Midwest totaled only $9.5

million.

Dick Schaak, the hotshot from Minneapolis, believed he could turn Allied's performance around. "Allied gave birth to this industry," Schaak told the *Chicago Tribune.* "It's still got a top name—and research we've done since the acquisition bears that out." By stressing brand names instead of private labels—a strategy taken by Tandy—Schaak believed he could recharge Allied's batteries.

Schaak told the *Tribune* reporter of a young couple that lusted after a $1,200 hi-fi system at one Allied store. "But they walked out without buying," Schaak said. "They came back Monday with the money. They sold their car. The potential in this business is fantastic."

A few persons close to Dick Schaak, however, warned him against such speedy expansion. "I worried about how Dick would come up with enough competent people to work those Allied Stores," says Jack Klein. "Dick had always trained people well before moving them into management slots. He had orderly, steady growth before the Allied acquisition. Then, all of a sudden, he doubled in size overnight. He had to tackle the cost of inventory for all those new stores, find staff, mount new marketing efforts, service the debt, absorb it all. Meanwhile, the country was buffeted by a double whammy—inflation and recession—in 1973, '74 and '75. Most people would have been afraid to make that move."

The doubts were well-founded. Schaak did act too soon and on too grand a scale. In addition, he had taken his eyes off the Schaak balance sheet, and poor financial controls surfaced the same year he decided to acquire Allied. As Schaak himself puts it, "I delegated and abdicated."

"I found $40,000 in checks in the accountant's office drawer, some of them a year old," he says. In an ironic link to 1960, when Schaak reviewed his father's books and found cash flow dangerously lacking, he discovered similar problems in his own operation. "Our accounts receivable were a mess," he recalls. "We found we had to write off $250,000 in receivables alone." Schaak's billing system had allowed customers to cart out stereo system after stereo system without a payment.

Those poor controls coupled with the added financial burden of the Allied acquisition sent Schaak Electronics into a tailspin. "I went into 1974," Schaak says, "without ever having any financial problems and without a single loss year. At first, it never occurred to me that we could possibly be in financial trouble. When you're on a roll and you think you have the golden touch, it never seems that things could fall apart.''

□ But fall apart they did. In fiscal 1974, Schaak Electronics lost $771,775 compared with a net gain of $290,028 a year earlier. Sales increased by 42.9 percent in 1974, but earnings dropped to zero. In 1975, Schaak sales increased by 37.6 percent, but the corporation lost $1.32 million.

Schaak quickly set about cutting his losses. He closed 17 Allied stores and two Schaak outlets around the country; most of the closed stores were at some geographic distance from the Twin Cities. "We had some stores that were very profitable, but they were in areas too hard to control," Schaak explains. "The Ann Arbor store was just six months old. We hadn't even paid for remodeling when we closed it. In one month, that store had run up more than $100,000 in business. It wasn't an easy decision. There were healthy vital signs in Ann Arbor. But we had to cut our total dollars paid in rent; we had to cut salaries; we had to consolidate our inventory in fewer stores."

Schaak's public statements still conveyed echoes of the old confidence. "This is *not* a going out of business sale!" a boldfaced newspaper ad declared in Chicago. In small type, the ad said: "We are closing our stores in Skokie and Hillsdale so that we can create large electronic supermarkets in our remaining locations." So much for optimism.

If anyone needed a shot of confidence at the time, it was the American National Bank of St. Paul and Manufacturers Hanover Trust Company in New York. Officers at both institutions were worried about the losses Schaak Electronics posted in 1974.

A meeting that Dick Schaak, his attorney Patrick O'Neill and Schaak's vice president of finance attended December 17, 1974, in St. Paul was expected to be perfunctory. Schaak Electronics was a solid bank customer—the company made timely loan payments, kept a comfortable balance and met all of its capital requirements. John Barry, senior vice president and chief lending officer at American National, had even written a letter recommending Dick Schaak as St. Paul's Outstanding Young Man of the Year two years earlier. Barry had offered glowing words in that recommendation: "During the past 11 years in the Schaak Electronics business, this man has taken one store with $140,000 annual sales volume and built it into a chain of 10 stores with $4,000,000 annual sales volume. In building the chain of electronics stores, it was necessary to obtain a strong banking relationship, and in doing so, our bank has become over the years, the lead bank for the Schaak organization...[we] have found that Dick Schaak is a man of the highest integrity and with character above reproach."

All the same, that December 17th meeting at American National turned out to be no love feast.

"We walked in at 2 o'clock simply expecting to sign new letters of credit [to help finance Schaak expansion]," Patrick O'Neill recalls. "Instead, we walked into a room with some 25 people. Representatives of American National were there. Representatives of Manufacturers Hanover were there. Attorneys representing both banks were there. We left at midnight—10 hours later—and when we left, Schaak Electronics was wiped out."

American National and Manufacturers Hanover held $2.5 million in Schaak notes. Both banks informed Schaak that he would no longer have a line of credit. Furthermore, both banks took control of the company's bank account to recoup an anticipated loss. "Overnight we went from solvency to insolvency when the banks pulled our funds," Schaak says.

"That was the *first* shock to Dick," says Howard Patrick, a St. Paul attorney specializing in "corporate rehabilitation [reorganization and Chapter 11 proceedings]." "When I first met him, I don't think Dick had experienced any kind of failure. He was bright and hard-driving and ambitious, but he was also naive. This action by the banks was a total shock. He considered this a failure, and I think he was personally embarrassed. His whole world had been a series of successes and upward moves. All of a sudden, life was not rosy."

In retrospect, Patrick believes that both the lenders and Schaak erred on the side of optimism: "I think the lending officers who worked with Dick from day to day liked him personally. They saw Schaak as a great account, and they saw it as an up-and-coming business. They wanted to help

Dick. But the people who told Dick to go ahead with his building plans weren't the top people who finally called the shots in December 1974. Perhaps the underling lenders overstepped their authority...and Dick had assumed that everything was okay.

"As bright and talented as Dick Schaak was in 1974, his company was growing much too fast for him to continue to handle every aspect of it," Patrick continues. "And he was still trying to do that. He had not learned to surround himself with talent. Dick felt he could keep his finger on the pulse of the company and still know everything that was going on. But he simply couldn't. Schaak Electronics was growing too big."

Schaak, Patrick and O'Neill met with the lenders a few days after that December 17th meeting and reached a temporary agreement. The banks would continue to finance day-to-day operations as long as Schaak Electronics was restructured and Schaak paid his creditors. Schaak Electronics had been current on all of its obligations to creditors, Patrick says, but once the banks froze the Schaak account, the company could pay no bills.

A creditors' committee was formed and agreed not to force Schaak's existing obligations. From January 1975 through early spring of that year, Dick Schaak walked on eggs. He also searched his soul.

"When a company finds it has financial problems, it's always due to mismanagement—the president didn't do his job," he says. "It's easy to blame other people—employees or some institution that you're doing business with. That might be a darn good crutch, but it isn't honest. I had the power to change institutions, to fire bad personnel, to quit doing business with certain people. I had the power...but I didn't exercise it. I delegated...but I also abdicated."

"The Thursday before Easter [1975], I had a long discussion with an attorney representing Manufacturers Hanover," says Howard Patrick. "He was concerned about an apparent discrepancy of inventory in some Schaak stores. There was talk of employee theft, but it was a matter of loose record-keeping. Manufacturers Hanover was concerned, so I said to their attorney, 'Don't push the panic button, and don't do anything until you call me first and we discuss it.'

"The next day was Good Friday," says Patrick. "About 3:30 I got a call from the attorney representing American National. 'Are you sitting down?' he asked.

" 'Yes,' I said.

" 'We just pulled all the money out of the Schaak account,' he said. 'About three million dollars.' The company's inventory would be next."

Patrick told Schaak to open another business account immediately, so funds filtering in from retail stores could not be claimed by American National or Manufacturers Hanover. Patrick and Schaak then filed for reorganization and protection of the courts under Chapter 11 of the federal bankruptcy law. Schaak Electronics' net worth had sunk to $100,000. At one point Schaak owed $4.2 million to two banks, American National and Manufacturers Hanover.

Over the next two years, Dick Schaak was enmeshed in an intense, bitterly fought struggle. Two banks and about 30 major creditors were after him. He wrestled with personal doubt and unflattering public attention. Dick Schaak—the man named one of Minnesota's 10 Outstanding Young Men and Entrepreneur of the Year by Harvard University—was on the skids. Even the family felt the sting. "Ah, Kimmy," a grade school teacher said in loud voice to Dick's nine-year-old daughter. "I hear that your daddy is bankrupt and going to jail."

Fortunately, St. Paul bankruptcy judge Jacob Dim ruled that Schaak Electronics could make use of new sales and receivables it generated during this rocky period. He determined that the banks were adequately secured and could not lay claim to Schaak's funds.

Schaak quickly set to work cutting back his operating expenses. He had to demonstrate to the judge and his creditors that he could conserve and succeed. Only at a lean, trim fighting weight did Schaak Electronics have a chance. Cost-cutting meant new tasks, among other things. "He terminated all his janitorial staff," says Howard Patrick, "and he assigned each one of his executives, including himself, one night a week to clean the offices. Dick figured he could save $20,000 a year that way."

As well as running the company, Schaak was meeting with creditors around the country and shaping the reorganization of his company. "He didn't walk into my office and say, 'Here's my problem, you solve it,' " says Howard Patrick. "Dick was involved in this 24 hours a day. He made major contributions—he saved his own company. He simply called in the mechanics like me to help him do it. He was hurting and suffering, but at no time did I see him beaten."

□ There were several offers during those hard times to buy the distressed enterprise, and, like it or not, Schaak had to entertain them all. Schaak owed a major vendor $400,000. "The president of that firm called and said he was flying out with some officers of his company to close the loan," Schaak recalls. "He said he'd save me from this deep trouble if I'd put up all my stock [54 percent ownership] and sell it to them for $1. Not $1 a share, but $1 for the 54 percent. He offered me a management contract and the opportunity to buy back shares in Schaak Electronics up to three percent.

"I listened quietly to the whole thing. I told him he was well-meaning, but I believed I had to go it alone. Nor would I give up any equity in my company. I truly believed we had the strength to work this out ourselves."

The chief suitor left, but the man's financial vice president lingered behind to offer Schaak some parting words. "Nobody does this to Mr. X," the vice president said. "I guarantee that you won't get out of this trouble without giving up equity in this company." "Between the lines his message was this," Schaak says. " 'We're going to see that you don't come out of this whole.' It was the best thing he could have said to me. That threat made me more determined than ever."

Schaak considered no fewer than 13 acquisition proposals over two-and-a-half years. "I listened to guys who came out of the woodwork," he says. "Guys with their hair slicked back, wearing thousand-dollar suits and dripping with jewelry. Guys who laid out schemes telling me I could walk away from all this with at least $750,000 in my pocket. Guys on the lookout for someone in trouble. Buyers of distressed merchandise. Junk dealers. Well, even in the worst of times, I didn't see Schaak Electronics in *that* category."

Schaak seriously considered at least one offer, however.

It came from the CMC Corporation of St. Louis, another retail electronics firm. The real carrot for Schaak was CMC's willingness to continue a $95-million lawsuit Schaak had brought against both American National Bank and Manufacturers Hanover. "My great desire was to nail the banks," Schaak says. "It really played on my mind." The action, though many observers believed Schaak had a strong-enough case, was reminiscent of the 110-pound high school kid taking on the 180-pound bully. When CMC decided it would not continue the litigation, Schaak saw no reason to sell.

Schaak, meanwhile, fought off creditors who wanted part ownership in his company. "I flatly refused because I was offering them 100 cents on a dollar. I was not offering them a fraction of the debt, but the *entire* debt. I didn't feel they had any ownership rights. This delayed discussions and our eventual settlement, but we did stick by our guns. There was no dilution in ownership of any of our stockholders, including myself. I owned 54 percent of the company before *and* after the troubles."

Dick Schaak does not have steel nerves, but during the "troubles" he behaved as if he did. "It was important to me not to let anyone, including my wife, know, but I was in big trouble inside," he says now. "Not employees, not attorneys, not friends—I didn't want them to see me in the valley. As president of a company I believe no matter how you feel, you can't show it. If you look down, your employees are going to start feeling down, and that's when they'll leave you. If you tell your attorney, it might change his thinking. If you tell one of your fellow officers, you might lose some of his confidence. If you have any doubts, you really can't express them to anybody."

But in the midst of this self-imposed isolation, Schaak finally decided to look outward. "I decided I had to talk to someone on a daily basis, and I had to have help in making decisions," he explains. "I chose God."

Schaak does not tell this part of his story with evangelistic fervor. He does not describe himself as a "born-again" Christian. He does not preach the Gospel from executive row. But he is not shy about explaining what happened late one night in "the valley":

"I had a habit of reading myself to sleep. It was a fitful night, so I picked up the Bible believing that would do it. I didn't know how to read the Bible, so I started at page one, Genesis. The story tells about this guy, God, who decides to get something going on earth—a real entrepreneur, you see. He makes Adam and Eve, and he puts them in Paradise, but there are a couple rules and regulations they must obey. Well, Adam and Eve get a little puffed up and start believing their good life is on *their* account. So they bend the rules. Then God gives the world written rules to live by. He etches that policy in stone and calls it the Ten Commandments. But mankind still breaks the rules. This time, God gathers his key people together, puts them on a boat and floods the earth. He closes the hatch, leaves the flotsam behind, and when the ship comes to rest after 40 days, he starts all over again.

"At 3 o'clock in the morning, that was God's way of telling me life has its ups and downs. When you get into trouble, you gather your resources, get your ship afloat and start over again. This time you make it. Things may get messy, but you make it. You have a partner."

Schaak attended mass every morning during his two years of reorganization. He had a message for his "partner": "Just guide me in the right direction; I won't give up and I won't let you down." Finally, the skies began to brighten.

Schaak dropped his suit against American National and Manufacturers Hanover Trust when the banks agreed in 1976 to extend a loan and to fund a plan to repay the company's creditors. And within two years of an eight-year scheduled payment plan at eight percent interest, Schaak repaid his creditors and began rebuilding. Then Schaak Electronics posted $836,998 in profits for fiscal 1976 on sales of $14.9 million. In 1978, those figures were $1.3 million in profits on sales of $31.2 million. The company, moreover, now has a $4.5-million unsecured line of credit from American National, and Schaak has been elected to the bank's board of directors.

"Building a business is like raising a child," says Schaak's wife Pat. "You nurture it. You put so much of your life into it. In those earlier years, we referred to the company as if it were some living, breathing thing. Since Chapter 11, Dick has decided the business had to be a smaller part of his life. He decided he wouldn't invest that much again in an entity that wasn't even human."

Dick Schaak now directs some of his intensity to sports—individual sports like handball and scuba-diving. He has become a student of photography, and he reads extensively. "Dick believes that once a person quits learning, he has begun to die," says his wife. "He's infected with a pervasive need to know. He's a seeker—and he knows more subjects than management theory and audio marketing.

"Since Chapter 11, Dick has mellowed. He enjoys himself more. He still goes in early and brings work home, but he works smarter. Weekends, without exception, are reserved for the family."

"Most business people go through their entire careers on pins and needles, wondering what would happen if the going got tough," Dick Schaak says. "I feel fortunate that I've had this question answered early. I know now that if our company were to face another crisis, I would have the fortitude to see it through. I've learned the areas of business that I'm good at and those I'm not good at. And, by identifying those differences, I've hired people strong in the areas where I'm weak. Today our potential for growth is much greater than it was prior to our financial calamity."

Dick Schaak appears to be a rare exception in a field of entrepreneurs driven by an insatiable appetite for achievement and power in single-minded pursuit of business success. Still in his 40s, he has learned a lesson about balance that comes late in the lives of many entrepreneurs—if at all. And the single most important catalyst in the greening of Dick Schaak was his "financial calamity."

Today he wears a heavy gold-and-gemstone ring on his finger. A stylized tree is carved in the metal. "When we were coming out of Chapter 11," he says, "I was in Kyoto, Japan, on business. I asked about a tree I saw growing near the Panasonic plant. It had slim limbs reaching for the sky. It looked like sculpture. My guide called it the 'Tree of the Hungry Spirit.' "

Dick Schaak planted another tree on the grounds.

"I recognized my own hungry spirit," he says. "I had to grow. I was never satisfied. I had to accomplish more. I still feel that way. But like a tree needing nourishment to grow, I also need nourishment in the form of wisdom, spiritual growth and now balance."

Rose Totino

8

Rose Totino

Big Business in the Kitchen

When Peter Cruciani lost his job with the city in 1928, it was his daughter Rose, age 13, who went to talk to the mayor.

A new ordinance had banned all but "full-fledged" citizens from holding city jobs, and Peter Cruciani was not a "full-fledged" citizen. He did not yet have those all-important final papers. In the meantime, there were seven hungry mouths to feed.

It was a long streetcar ride from northeast Minneapolis to the great stone City Hall on Fourth Street. Clutching return fare in her hand, Rose climbed the steps and made her way down the wide hallway to the mayor's office.

The tears and the words poured out together. "My father was laid off because he doesn't have his second paper, but he's going to get it," she said. "Isn't there some kind of work he can do—even just part-time—so we can buy food?"

It would have taken a harder heart than Mayor George Leach's to resist this plea. "We'll send out a social worker," he said, writing down her family's name and address.

"Oh, no, we can't accept anything like that," Rose interrupted. "He wants to work. We won't take charity."

Ordinance or not, Peter Cruciani was called back to work that winter. Soon afterward, he had his citizenship papers, and he held the city job until he retired. And the social worker did come, Rose remembers, not to dispense food or clothing—"charity"—but to ask if any of the Cruciani children wanted to take piano lessons. "I did," Rose says. "Of course, we didn't have a piano, but we did have radiators. I labeled a radiator C,D,E,F,G,A,B,C, and when I practiced, I played the radiator."

No one has ever accused Rose Totino of being unresourceful. In their mid-30s, she and her husband Jim opened an Italian restaurant on a hunch, a $1,500 loan, her mother's recipes and plenty of determination. Ten years later, they invested their life's savings in a frozen-food plant. The first year they almost went under, but they survived and eventually prospered. In 1976, they sold that frozen-food business for more than $20 million in stock to the Pillsbury Company, where Rose Totino is now the first woman vice president in the company's 110-year history.

Rose Totino is quick to say that she's had no formal training in management or business. What she does have is perhaps even more important than classroom learning: the values instilled in her by her parents, her own considerable intelligence and a complete faith in the ability of the people she hires. She calls it common sense.

□ Fourth in a family of seven, Rose Totino had responsibility early. Her parents, Peter and Armita Cruciani, emigrated from Italy in 1910. They joined other Italians in Pennsylvania, where there was work in the coal mines. But for Peter, who had herded sheep in the hills of northern Italy, working underground was like being buried alive. So, after Armita's sister settled in Minneapolis, Peter moved the family to Minnesota. Peter found work with the city, paving streets with tar in the summer and shoveling snow in the winter. The family settled in the Italian neighborhood of northeast Minneapolis, where in 1915, Rose was born.

The Crucianis had seven children in all. Armita managed her brood with authority and affection. She instilled her values in each of them: be honest, respect your elders, and never take anything that doesn't belong to you. From morning to night, while Peter maintained city streets, Armita kept her house clean, her garden growing, her children clothed and the family fed. To say it wasn't easy is an understatement.

In the spring, Armita planted the garden that would provide vegetables throughout the year. Late in the summer, she dried herbs and beans and canned tomatoes. Through the mid-1920s, there was still room in northeast Minneapolis for flocks of chickens and a few head of livestock for each family. Peter raised a pig every year, and Armita rendered lard while he supervised the sausage-making. A cow provided milk, but not for the family. Rose's job was to sell the milk—at five cents a quart—to the neighbors. That cow brought in 75 cents a day, or more than $5 a week toward clothing and shoes for the growing Cruciani children. Any milk left over was made into cheese to grate over the pasta that was a household staple.

Peddling milk was not Rose's only job. When Armita covered her head with a big, white kerchief, Rose knew it was bread-making day. That meant she had to hurry home from school to wash the big pan her mother used for kneading the dough. If Rose lingered, the dough would dry out and the job would be a tough one. Bread-making day also meant a treat for the Cruciani children. Armita reserved enough dough to make individual thin-crust pizzas for everyone. She spread the adults' pizzas with tomatoes and herbs, but she sprinkled the children's with cinnamon and sugar. It was the only dessert the family could afford.

"I'm glad I had the experience of being poor," Rose Totino says now. "It gave me compassion for other people. I know what it's like to have seven kids share one bike, one nickel for the Sunday-school collection. I never had a doll—I dressed a milk bottle. That's how poor we were. There were times when I went to bed hungry. I'll never forget how angry with me my mother was when I complained about not having enough to eat. She was doing the best she could—keeping us fed and clothed was a full-time job.

"But I had a beautiful childhood," she adds. "Mother was always there."

Armita's steady presence was not her only legacy. The simple diet of home-grown foods, carefully rationed meat and limited sweets is undoubtedly responsible for Rose Totino's good health and seemingly limitless energy. And at Armita's side, Rose learned about making pasta and other Italian foods that would someday be the basis of her business.

From her father, Rose learned to enjoy life. "My dad was so happy-go-lucky," she says. "He was always singing, no matter how tired he was. When he came home from work, he would stick his head in the door and say hello, then go right downstairs to the wine barrel. He never missed a day of work and he never was drunk, but he did enjoy the wine. We kids grew up drinking small glasses of wine mixed half-and-half with water."

Rose has a favorite story about her parents. "One day when I was in the third grade," she recalls, "some of the kids at school were saying that the world was going to end that night at midnight. I went home sobbing with fear. When I walked in the door, my mother asked what was the matter. I said, 'Mom, the world is going to end tonight—the kids at school are all talking about it.' "

"If that's the case," Armita said, "when we get through with supper, we had better all kneel down and pray."

"I went out to the barn," Rose continues, "where my dad was milking the cow. 'What's the matter, Rosinella?' he asked. 'Dad,' I said, 'tonight at midnight the world is going to end. The kids are all talking about it.' "

"If that's the case," said Peter Cruciani, "we'd better finish the barrel of wine."

"That," says Rose Totino, "was the difference between my mother and my dad."

☐ Although Rose was a bright student, she left school at 16 to go to work. "Mother felt it was more important for the boys to be educated," she says. "She felt that we girls didn't need an education for what God put us on this earth to do—to be wives and mothers. So I quit school to do housework for $2.50 a week. With my $2.50 a week and my sister's $2.50, my mother could buy groceries for the family. And our brothers could stay in school."

Before long, Rose found a better job than housework—working at the Hollywood Candy factory for 17 cents an hour. She was a quick and eager worker and was soon earning the magnificent wage of 37 cents an hour—

almost $15 a week.

At night, Rose went dancing with her friends, often at the Viking Dance Hall near downtown Minneapolis. It was there that she met a young baker, Jim Totino, who had also left school at 16 to help support his family. At 19, Rose married the 23-year-old Totino and settled down to do what God had put her on earth to do.

It's not surprising that Rose Totino became involved in the community. The family lived across the street from an elementary school, and the Totino house became a favorite after-school pizza stop. PTA meetings often ended there, too. Although she had no sons, Rose was a Boy Scout den mother, and her young Scouts were occasionally treated to pizza. Before long, friends began asking Rose to cater their parties.

"I hated to take money from friends," she recalls. "But they told me they wouldn't feel they could ask me a second time if I didn't take pay." Their friends also urged the Totinos to open a shop where they could come and buy pizza whenever they wanted it.

"Jim and I talked and talked about opening a shop. We knew there were pizzerias in Chicago and New York, but here in Minnesota pizza was unknown. We thought it just might catch on. So we began looking for a little place to rent. We decided that if we could get some good used equipment, we could probably open up for about $1,500. Of course, that was $1,500 we didn't have."

The next step was finding collateral for a bank loan. "We did have a car that was about three years old, but we were still paying on it," Rose says. "We didn't want to take a chance on losing our home—we were paying on that, too—so we didn't really know what to do. I called Central Northwestern Bank to talk to the president about a loan. When I told him we wanted to open a pizza place, he said, 'Pizza? What's that?' So I baked a pizza and took it with me when I went to see him."

The banker agreed to the $1,500 loan, with the car as collateral. And, on February 7, 1951, Rose and Jim opened the door of Totino's Italian Kitchen at Central and East Hennepin in northeast Minneapolis. Neither one was prepared for the response. The Totinos had advertised by passing out samples in the new frozen-food department of Donaldsons' downtown Minneapolis department store, and they had done a good job. Almost immediately, customers lined up outside the Totinos' door.

They had planned to sell their food on a take-out basis only. "We had hot and frozen pizza and spaghetti," Rose says. "We had shelves of dry pastas and imported foods. But there weren't many restaurants in the neighborhood, and at noon, when the boys from the filling station came in and ordered hot spaghetti, they would ask for a fork and eat it right there standing up. I decided to put up a couple of cardtables so they could sit down. We brought in another cardtable and then another, and pretty soon the place was *full* of cardtables. I said, 'Jim, we're running a restaurant, and we'd better get with it.' We threw out the freezers and the shelving, went to Aslesens [a restaurant supplier] for furnishings and began running a restaurant."

Jim, in the meantime, had kept his job at the bakery. "We hoped that in about a year the business would be big enough for him to take over so I could stay home and be a wife and mother," Rose says. But she never got the chance. Within a week of their opening, Rose was asked to demonstrate the mysteries of pizza-making on Arlie Haeberle's local television show. "And I couldn't even make a motion at a PTA meeting without breaking out in a cold sweat," she recalls.

Pizza was a novelty that caught on quickly, and Totino's Italian Kitchen was an instant success. "I figured that if we could sell 25 big pizzas a week at $1.25 each, we could pay the $85-a-month rent," Rose says. "At first, we weren't sure whether we were making any money or not. We worked so hard and such long hours that we didn't even have time to count the money. All we knew was that after we paid the breadman, the milkman and the help, we had money left over."

The Totinos' first employees were family members, including Jim's sister, Mary DeMay, who "just came down to help because she was interested" and still works part-time at the restaurant. Thirteen-year-old Joanne Totino did her homework there and waited tables at suppertime. Two-year-old Bonnie took her naps curled up in the corner of a booth.

Within three months, Jim Totino said good-by to the bakery and began baking pizzas—120 or more a day—in the kitchen of their restaurant. Rose and Jim worked side by side, he baking the pizzas and she applying the topping. Using Armita Cruciani's recipe, they experimented, adding mozzarella cheese and Italian sausage to the tomato sauce and herbs. Jim went to Chicago to learn how veterans in the business were making pizzas. Instead of sliced sausage, he decided, he would cook sausage in open kettles and sprinkle it on the pies.

There was more to running a restaurant than serving food, the Totinos discovered. "I realized we had better get organized and start keeping track of what we were doing," Rose says. "We started saving all the cash register tapes and putting the date on each one. Then we started hiring people."

Jim and Rose Totino put in 10 years of 18- to 20-hour days in that restaurant. On weekends, the busiest days, they would make 400 to 500 pizzas—and still run out. They stayed open until 2 a.m., often tying a rope across the door to keep the restaurant from becoming impossibly crowded. When the roofing contractor next door went out of business, the Totinos rented the space and doubled their seating capacity. In 1956, they bought the building and began making improvements—a gas furnace and new flooring to replace the multicolored linoleum that was wearing thin in patches.

By 1961, the Totinos had saved $50,000, and it was time to make a decision. "We talked about retiring," Rose remembers. "But we were still young—Jim was only 45—and we were used to working." The restaurant had proved beyond doubt that pizza was here to stay. Now they realized that a market existed for frozen, bake-at-home pizza and that the only product available in supermarkets was Chef Boy-Ar-Dee's. Jim and Rose thought theirs was better. They began thinking about producing frozen pizza in quantity. Late in 1961, they found a location—a former Mrs. Wolf's Salad Dressing plant in nearby St. Louis Park.

But producing frozen pizzas in quantity required a crust bakery, and the Totinos didn't have enough cash. "Why not start with frozen Italian entrees?" Rose wondered. When they accumulated enough capital, they could install the bakery and begin producing pizza. So, with the $50,000 they had saved, they made a down payment on the $140,000 plant and purchased the necessary equipment: a freezer, meat-cooking equipment, a pasta-maker, packaging equipment and a conveyer.

This time, the Totinos thought they were going into business with their eyes open. They incorporated, established a board of directors, and asked for advice. They started with two frozen pasta entrees, manicotti and mostaccioli, and an $80,000 advertising campaign—on advice that nearly cost them their business. They began production in January 1962, and by summer's end they had lost $150,000. "We were on the verge of bankruptcy," Rose says. "We had invested our life's savings from 10 years of blood and sweat and tears in the restaurant. When Jim told me we would have to file bankruptcy, I said, 'Jim, we just can't do it. My mother and my father taught us that we had to be honest and pay our bills. I can't file bankruptcy even if I have to take in washing the rest of my life. We'll have to work this out.' "

Work it out they did. That fall, Jim attended a frozen-food convention in Dallas, where he learned about pre-baked crusts. He came back from that convention with new enthusiasm. He said, "Rose, we can get into the pizza business without the bakery after all. All we need is some new packaging equipment, and I think we can get that for about $50,000." "Using frozen crusts was an opportunity to salvage our company," Rose says, "to get us out of the hole we were in. We would use them to start with, but I figured someday I would build my own bakery and make crusts like my mother made."

Again, the Totinos needed money they didn't have. They applied for a Small Business Administration loan. The loan was granted on the basis of the restaurant's success and the Totinos' management of the business. This time, the Totinos put everything they had on the line: their home, a lake cottage, even some property they had acquired in Carver County. They agreed to take no salary from the plant until the loan was repaid.

Rose set about developing recipes. "I never did like those pre-baked crusts from Chicago; I thought they were just like cardboard. But Jim said that three or four other companies were using them, and they appeared to be successful. 'Well,' I said, ' since we're all using the same crusts, we'll just have to figure out how *we* can make a better topping.' "

Jim Totino worked on a method for dispensing pizza sauce. According to Rose, "He came to work one morning with an old phonograph player. He put the crust on the turntable so the sauce could be distributed evenly as the crust turned. It worked, but we got a shock every time we touched the thing." Eventually Rose designed more sophisticated machines for dispensing pizza sauce, but she and her employees continued to apply the pizza toppings—sausage and cheese—by hand.

A marketing system was the next challenge. Rose knew that selling Totino's pizza in Minnesota would be relatively simple. It was, at that time, the only one available. "We thought about going after Chicago, the next logical step geographically. But we knew it was a dog-eat-dog environment and that the cost of advertising would be too high. So our next market was Denver."

Rose was learning fast. "I took an oven and a pizza and went out to talk to the Denver broker, but he was selling Fox Deluxe [a regional brand] and wouldn't even see us. 'Who needs another pizza?' he asked. 'Denver is not a pizza market—our total sales here are only 1,500 cases a month.' I told him we would help him build a pizza market in Denver—after all, if he could sell only 1,500 cases a month, we wouldn't be interested. He did take our product, and now we sell half a million cases a year there. It's one of our biggest markets."

□ Within three months, the Totinos knew they had a success. They also knew they needed help. "We couldn't even read a profit-and-loss statement," Rose remembers. "The first time the bank called to ask for a cash-flow statement, I said, 'There's no cash flowing around here!' " More lessons—cash flow and balance sheets and all the other aspects of a business that grows faster than its founders dreamed. "We were going to be opening up markets thousands of miles away, and I realized we had to have a marketing department," Rose says. "We had to think about designing the packages and cartons and getting approval for the label. I knew I wasn't qualified to handle all of that. So I began by hiring some marketing people, along with a bookkeeper and plant manager."

The Totinos were stunned by the revenues their company was earning. "In the third or fourth month of operation, we made $100,000,'' Rose says. "I went out to the plant and announced, 'Let's put a little extra meat on each pizza. We don't have to make all that money.' "

Rose and Jim had made a decision—"to go for broke"—and they were going to make it. They expanded the plant twice and outgrew the expansions as soon as they were occupied. By 1970, the Totinos knew they needed larger facilities. They went to the bank for another loan, this time to finance a new $2.5-million plant, including a bakery, in Fridley, a north Minneapolis suburb. Rose expanded the administrative work force as well, hiring a president. She turned her own attention to quality control, making sure their product was as much like her home-baked pizza as she could make it. "We didn't have a quality-control laboratory, so my job from day one was to taste all the ingredients to see that they were right—that the tomatoes were sweet enough, the sausage not too fat. And, of course, I sat in on all staff meetings. We built a real team."

It didn't happen overnight, however. The first president didn't work out, nor did the second. After some false starts, Rose found people who felt about the business as she did. The "Totino team" was thus forged. "Around Rose you have a feeling that things are going to work out," says Rod Miley, who began as vice president of marketing and served as president from 1974 to 1976. "Just about everyone who worked there feels it was the best place we've ever worked. We'd do it again in a minute."

Richard Nickel, now a vice president at Pillsbury, joined Totino's Finer Foods as a marketing manager. He describes the loyalty that he and the other members of the team felt. "The Totinos gave us 100 percent responsibility," he says. "We never thought about doing anything that would somehow reflect poorly on the company. For that reason, the Totinos got the best out of their employees."

"She's extremely bright and intuitive," Miley says of Rose. "She has the ability to size up people and choose the ones she can trust. She gives them complete authority. You'd die before you'd mess up her business."

Implicit trust sums up Rose Totino's management style. "I never have ruled with an iron hand," she says. "I find that if you tell people what you expect of them and that you depend on them, they will do the job. When the marketing man would come to me with Plan A and Plan B and ask me which we should use, I would tell him I didn't know anything about marketing, that it was his business and he had to tell me which was best—that was why I'd hired him. I told our employees we would give them whatever they needed to execute their plans, but making the decisions was their responsibility. It worked every time. There was no passing the buck, because if the marketing man had made that decision, he would work darned hard to make sure it worked. When you give them the reins, I've found, people will come through every time.''

It was a technique the Totinos learned the hard way. ''The first big piece of equipment Jim and I bought for the St. Louis Park plant,'' Rose recalls, ''we ordered without asking our production man what he thought. Well, the machine never worked because the production man was not consulted. It was a blow to him to think we would go buy a machine without talking to him first. We never did it again. From then on, when we needed to make a decision, we consulted the people who would be affected by it.''

Rose Totino also learned about motivating employees. ''It's a terrible thing to undermine people,'' she says, simply. It is a fundamental tenent of human relations that Rose Totino understands instinctively. The Totinos had no sons, and, according to Dick Nickel, ''it turned out that most of the management staff was men—except for Carol Hanson, the purchasing agent. So we were Rose's boys. I don't think there was anyone older than 35—a young, aggressive group of people. And none of us wanted to let her or the family down.''

Managers hired by the Totinos in those crucial years had to control a business that seemed to be growing in every direction at once. ''In many ways, it was like having a tiger on the end of a 100-foot rope,'' Nickel says. ''When a business is growing that fast, the real challenge is internal management. Being able to process all the paperwork, meet government regulations and do all the other things necessary to keep afloat.''

Beginning in about 1972, everything started to spin, Nickel recalls. ''We had to put some planning and discipline into the organization, to computerize the accounting system, to make the necessary improvements in the plant so we could keep up with demand. Everyone had to give 110 percent, and we all worked together. There were never any sessions where one person would point a finger at another for having dropped the ball, because we all knew that the next day it could be our turn.

"It taught us to do the right things and do them well, because there was entirely too much to do. We learned to do only what really mattered to the business, to help it grow. At the same time, there was great demand for accuracy, because a small mistake—a $50,000 mistake—could have sent the company down and taken our jobs with it. It made us understand risk."

The new plant had three times the capacity of the old—and many more times the overhead. In order to keep it running, Totino's had to open new markets, but opening new markets took money. "We were walking a tightrope," Rod Miley says, "turning money fast enough to keep up with the increasing orders. It made good managers out of us."

It was Rose Totino, as chief executive officer, who kept a steady eye on production, markets and growth. She was also thinking about the future and about the decisions that again had to be made. She says, "I had surrounded myself with a good team, but they weren't going to be happy just running this plant to see how much money we could make. They wanted to build new plants and keep going. I had to keep things challenging for them. And in the back of my mind, I was thinking about developing more of my mother's recipes. I knew I could never accomplish that if I didn't have a good food engineering and technology department and the right resources. But we just didn't have it. Our profits went into growth, not into research and development."

Rose and Jim Totino were by then in their early 60s. Years earlier when they were still in the St. Louis Park plant, Jim's health had begun to fail, and Rose had assumed greater and greater responsibility. They had to decide whether to stay and grow or to sell the business.

By 1975, the company had settled down, Rod Miley says. Volume was increasing steadily, and new markets were opened. The next step would be a second plant in a more centralized location—and investment of another $8 million or $9 million. The Fridley plant was producing at capacity, and the Totinos knew they would have to either build another or sell out.

The management team put together an evaluation of the business and went looking for a buyer. There were plenty of suitors, including some of the largest food companies in the country. The Totinos eventually chose Pillsbury because it was a local company, Rose says, and because it believed in research and development. Pillsbury also had a national distribution network. So, in November 1975, when Totino's sales were more than $35 million a year, Pillsbury purchased the company in exchange for Pillsbury common stock valued at $22,190,000. And Rose Totino, at 60 years of age, became a corporate vice president.

It was the beginning of a new phase in her career. At first, she worked in research and development, but it became clear that she had other talents. Dick Nickel says that Rose Totino has emerged as the company's best sales person.

Soon after she joined Pillsbury, the company began work on improving the "cardboard crust" consumers (and Rose) complained about. Rose remembered the pizza crusts her mother had made from bread dough. After two years of research, Totino's brought out "Crisp Crust," based on Armita Cruciani's long-ago treats for her children. Pillsbury knew that Rose Totino was the person who could best introduce "Crisp Crust" to the nation. At the company's public-relations firm in New York, Rose underwent an intensive three-day training session—complete with videotaped practice interviews—before embarking on a talk-show tour of the country, "the most fun thing I've ever done," she says.

The food brokers who sell and distribute products were an important factor in the growth of Totino's Finer Foods. Rose appreciated those brokers, and they knew it. "When we were planning to enter a new market," she says, "we interviewed brokers and picked the one that was right for us. Then we listened to him because he knew more about the market than we did, more about the competition. Most companies just tell the brokers what to do. But we asked for their input, and then they had the responsibility. It was a partnership."

At Pillsbury, Rose has insisted on maintaining that partnership with brokers. Every 18 months, she takes a group of 50 brokers—winners of a sales competition—and their wives to Italy. The tour includes a day-long feast in the village where her mother was born. The 400 residents serve roast pig and lamb, homemade wine, bread and salami. The town band plays while Americans and Italians dance, eat together and make friends. "By the time we leave at the end of the day," Dick Nickel says, "there are tears in everyone's eyes."

☐ Rose Totino has covered a lot of ground in her career—from $2.50 a week as a high school dropout to vice president of a large corporation. But in fundamental ways, she has not changed. Jim Totino, who supported and encouraged her for so long, died in 1981. They lived in the same house in northeast Minneapolis for 37 years. She remembers her first extravagance—a pair of red shoes purchased when she and Jim were running the restaurant. She never had time to wear them. She did buy a pink Lincoln in 1957. ("I've had a pink Cadillac, too," she says, "but I think I like Lincolns better.")

Early in her business, Rose established a policy of giving five percent of pre-tax profits to charity. She and Jim formed a foundation, Charity, Inc., "to spread the good news of the Gospel through churches, youth organizations and schools, and to help people who are hurting." Jim Totino chose to give to a Roman Catholic high school near their Fridley plant, supporting a girl's volleyball team, building a theater, tennis courts and softball fields. The school is now named for the Totinos.

One year, Dick Nickel says, the foundation did not give away all the money in its fund. The money was invested, and it made a profit, almost by accident. The Internal Revenue Service came to call, and the auditor asked Rose for her Charity, Inc., books.

"When Rose came in with two grocery bags full of receipts, the IRS man was absolutely flabbergasted," Nickel says. "He took the two shopping bags and a few other records with him, and about a week later the office called back with the news that Charity, Inc., owed about $40,000 in back taxes. So Rose invited the auditor to come over and talk about it."

The auditor returned, this time on crutches because of

an injury. "It happened to be just before lunch," Nickel
says, smiling, "so Rose invited him to stay. They sat down,
had a little pizza, a little wine, a little more pizza and a little
more wine. Two-and-a-half hours later, he left with a case
of pizza under each arm. The tax bill had been reduced to
$5,000—and he'd left his crutches in the kitchen!"

Rose Totino has an uncanny ability, Nickel says, to talk
to everyone without pretense. She is genuinely interested in
other people. Yet she felt uncomfortable in the corporate
world. "When I first became part of the company, I had
all these invitations to meetings, and I always found 15
good reasons why I shouldn't go," she says. "To be
honest, I never felt I could make a contribution because I
wasn't knowledgeable enough.

"Sometimes, I feel very inadequate because I can't dic-
tate a letter and I don't know how to use a calculator.
When I have to write a letter, Deanna [her secretary] and I
have to get in a huddle because when a letter comes from
me, it has to be from the heart. It can never be a formal
business letter. Most of the time, I send hand-written
notes.

"I don't know how to use a dictating machine or a
calculator—although I can rattle off multiplication tables
like nothing. I can figure my bank balance. I just don't
know all those newfangled things...I have never taken the
time to learn. And computers blow my mind!"

Maybe so. Rod Miley recalls sitting across the table from
Rose at management meetings: "For somebody who
claims not to know much about numbers, she does pretty
well. She could sit down, look at a page full of numbers
and zero in on just the one you wished you didn't have to
talk about. 'What's that?' she'd ask. Rose has a relative
way of thinking about numbers. She instinctively knows
how they relate to one another."

Rose Totino's instincts have served her well indeed.

Manuel Villafana

9

Manuel Villafana

The Heart of the Matter

In the late 1920s, just before the Depression cast its pall over much of the world, a young couple left their home in the hills of Puerto Rico to seek a better life in the States.

Like many others, Joaquin and Elisa Villafana moved to New York City's Spanish Harlem, where the sound of their native tongue gave reassurance against bitter winds and harsh economic reality. They were, as one son remembers, the poorest of the poor. Jobs were scarce, particularly for laborers handicapped by a strange language and little education.

Through the 1930s the Villafanas struggled, living on the ground floor of a south Bronx tenement. They had three boys. Then, in 1940, a fourth boy, Manuel, was born. Elisa Villafana was 46 years old.

Soon afterward, when United States involvement in World War II became a certainty, the family moved to Bridgeport, Connecticut, where both parents and the older boys found defense industry work. That latecomer, Manny, spent his days in a nursery.

Even though there were steady jobs, the family had trouble making ends meet. The older boys drifted away, and Joaquin Villafana's paycheck didn't last long. There were days of no food, just black coffee; of scouting the neighborhood for morsels—a tomato or an apple—to feed a child until payday came.

When World War II and defense jobs ended, Elisa and her two remaining sons returned to Spanish Harlem. But the moves and failures spelled defeat for Joaquin, who stayed in Connecticut where he would die a few years later. Elisa, Manuel and Nelson were alone.

It was not a childhood calculated to nurture a successful entrepreneur.

In the next few years, Nelson Villafana worked for the Pennsylvania Railroad, and Elisa worked as a seamstress, leaving young Manny to look after himself. Ten years older than Manny, Nelson was father to his little brother—disciplinarian when Manny played hooky, a source of encouragement for facing challenges. "You're never going to make it if you don't try," Nelson would tell Manny.

Manny Villafana might have turned to the streets, like many boys his age. But he didn't. The determination of Elisa and Nelson was one factor. His own intelligence and optimism was another. The attention he received from his other older brothers counted, too. Nelson pawned his wife's engagement ring to buy Manny an electric train one Christmas—only to learn that the older brothers had chosen an identical gift.

Then, at age eight, Manny Villafana discovered Kips Bay Boys' Club, a long subway ride away in Manhattan. Two years later, he had his first job, handling gym equipment at Kips Bay for 40 cents an hour. Kips Bay became Manny Villafana's home, and Charlie McNiven, the club's director, became a surrogate father. McNiven remembers Villafana as energetic and determined, a table-tennis champion at 13 who soon stood out as a boy with promise. Manny attended summer camp on scholarships and put in eight-hour days at the club during the school year. He had no lack of ambition.

Villafana applied for admittance to Cardinal Hayes High School in the Bronx—considered one of the best in the city. He paid his own way even though at his family's income level, he could have attended tuition-free. Cardinal Hayes was an excellent choice; by graduation in 1958,

Villafana was well-schooled in math and science.

Villafana then enrolled at Manhattan College, supporting himself and contributing to the household by working nights at a liquor store. It was his last year of full-time schooling; at 19 he began working days at Radio Engineering Laboratories on Long Island and taking evening courses at RCA Institute and Hunter College.

At 23, Villafana applied for a laboratory job at Ethyl Corporation. At this interview, his eye was caught by the receptionist, Elaine Dzubak. He won both the job and the girl. In 26 days he and Elaine were engaged. But by their wedding day in October 1965, Villafana decided he wasn't earning as much as he needed at Ethyl to be "properly married." He applied for a job at Picker International, a distributor for medical-products companies, including Minnesota-based Medtronic. His bilingual ability made South American sales a natural, and Villafana's career in medical products was launched.

Before long, the 26-year-old's success attracted attention at Medtronic, and when the company formed an international division in 1967, Villafana became one of its first salesmen. In 1969, he gave up continental commuting. He moved to Argentina, opened a Latin American sales branch, built an organization, made and met ambitious projections, and, best of all, sold pacemakers. Villafana's fluent Spanish and sales ability made his work seem like no work at all. That taste of independence in Argentina was a lesson in self-knowledge, too. Manny learned to like being his own boss.

Villafana's Latin American tenure might have lasted longer, but an allergy-induced illness in his young son forced a return to the United States. By that time, his independent streak and two years free from corporate politics had made him a square peg at Medtronic. "There was," he recalls, "no suitable place for me." By his own admission, he was a difficult employee, a loner. "When I came back from South America no one wanted me, no one was able to handle me," he says. He was impatient and headstrong, and he moved fast. He was hard to keep up with and even harder to supervise. He was also successful. It seemed clear by that time that Manny Villafana had to be on his own.

☐ Villafana began making plans to establish an independent sales organization in Australia to represent Medtronic and other medical-products companies. Visas in hand, their furniture in shipping cartons, the Villafanas readied themselves for another adventure. Villafana wanted a seven-year commitment from Medtronic ("After all, Australia is a long way away," he reasoned), but Medtronic would agree to only three. The couple unpacked the furniture and slipped their visas into a drawer.

A friend at Medtronic who recognized Villafana's talents introduced him to Med General, a struggling young Twin Cities company founded to manufacture surgical lights. Med General had innovation, but no strong leadership. Villafana signed on as chief executive officer and began raising capital in April 1971.

Later that year, two former Medtronic colleagues, James Baustert and Tony Adducci, came to Villafana for advice. They wanted to start a company to make a simple hospital operating-room device that would protect against electrical shock. Meeting at Arthur's, a northeast Minneapolis restaurant, Villafana reviewed their plans. "There were so many manufacturers already doing what they wanted to do," Villafana remembers. Instead, he had another idea. Earlier, he had run into Wilson Greatbatch, a Buffalo, New York, engineer who had made the first implantable pacemakers and licensed them to Medtronic in 1960. Medtronic had just turned down Greatbatch's latest project, a lithium-iodide battery that would allow pacemakers to remain implanted—without replacement surgery —much longer than conventional mercury-zinc-powered units.

"In those days," says Wilson Greatbatch, "50 percent of the pacemakers had to be replaced surgically within two years. And of that 50 percent, four-fifths had to be replaced because the mercury-zinc battery failed." The lithium-iodide battery Greatbatch developed had a more reliable separation between the anode and the cathode. Unlike the mercury-zinc batteries, it didn't produce gas, and as a result it could be hermetically sealed. It also had a much higher voltage; one battery cell could be used instead of four.

"That's what you should be making," he told his friends. "A new kind of pacemaker."

Recognizing that the lithium-powered pacemaker might

be a product for Med General, Villafana offered it to his board of directors—a suggestion that must have seemed like sheer folly. Medtronic, the industry leader, had already seen Greatbatch's lithium battery and said no. Why should Med General take on a product the industry giant had rejected? Obviously, it couldn't be done.

That logic, however, did not sway Villafana. He began laying the groundwork for a new company with Baustert and Adducci, then asked to be released from his job at Med General. Baustert and Adducci were still at Medtronic, keeping their plans under wraps until they were sure of financial backing. "We did a lot of soul-searching," Baustert remembers. "We wondered if we could do it. We finally came to the conclusion that we could—and we'd be fools *not* to!"

Villafana, Baustert and Adducci named the new company Cardiac Pacemakers, Inc. (CPI), leaving no doubt about what business they were in. Villafana set about finding financing. Every day, from his "office"—a phone booth in the Minneapolis skyway system—he made call after call to investment bankers and attorneys. "I learned that an entrepreneur often gets slapped, but once in a while he gets kissed," he says today. "I was slapped many times. It was hard to find anyone who would even listen to me."

That January, in 1972, was long and cold. Villafana's wife was hospitalized with pneumonia. His child was ill. He had no paying job, he had refinanced his house to invest in CPI—and time was running out. Then, one Sunday, sitting in a pew at St. John the Baptist Church in New Brighton, Villafana found a prayer card describing St. Jude, the saint of hopeless causes, of things almost despaired of. Villafana thus found an ally.

A few days later, investment bankers at Craig-Hallum, Inc., a Minneapolis firm, agreed to underwrite Cardiac Pacemakers.

It was not the end of CPI's troubles, however. Barely organized and not yet financed, the fledgling company was faced with a lawsuit: Medtronic claimed that Villafana, Adducci, Baustert and Art Schwalm, also a former Medtronic employee, had founded CPI with confidential information and trade secrets spirited away from Medtronic. Later, Med General sued for loss of corporate opportunity. Although both suits were eventually settled out of court, they hung like a cloud over Villafana and the company he was trying to organize.

But Craig-Hallum had raised $450,000 at $4.50 a share, and there was work to do. Tucking a Greatbatch lithium battery and a balsa-wood model of a pacemaker in a suitcase, Villafana set out to sell his product. In February 1972, manufacturing began, and the following November the first CPI pacemaker was implanted in a human being.

It was, for Manny Villafana, a tension-filled year. The lawsuits compounded the personal worries—a newborn child in repeated surgery to remove a growth that threatened his life. "Many times, I felt like giving up," Villafana remembers. "If it hadn't been for friends who took the time to talk with me and to listen, I might have. We were having problems with the product, we were being sued, we were low on money. The competitors were saying we would give the industry a black eye, that our batteries would fail."

As it happened, the lithium batteries did *not* fail. Instead, they revolutionized the industry. CPI prospered and grew, and in that growth lay another lesson: Manny Villafana does not enjoy the endless detail of administration in a large corporation. "Eventually you realize you can't shoot from the hip the way you did when you were a small company," he explains. "You have to have programs and education. You have to show you're the leader and do things that are expected of the leaders. Sometimes that means changing people." It became increasingly clear that a corporate bureaucracy was not where Villafana belonged.

Early in 1976, Villafana left CPI. Physicians who had been his pacemaker customers repeatedly spoke of the need for a better artificial heart valve. The valves they were using were big and clumsy. They made already weak hearts work harder, and they often wore out. In addition, they made some patients vulnerable to strokes. Spotting the opportunity, Villafana remembered the patron saint he discovered in a church pew years earlier. He founded St. Judé Medical—manufacturer of a better heart valve.

"This time, I formed a company not to design a better product, but to improve on a product that already existed," he says. He and his designers decided to make the valve entirely of pyrolitic carbon, a material that proved to be the answer to the early valve problems. The material was chemically inert so heart tissue did not grow around it and obstruct the flow of blood. It was compatible with the body, and it was durable. They chose a bi-leaflet design (two discs that opened as blood moved through) "because we wanted to be different," Villafana says. "Well, our valve turned out not only to be different, but better."

This time, financing was not a problem for Villafana. Cardiac Pacemakers had become a multimillion-dollar company, and investors who plunked down $4.50 a share in 1972 had seen their money double by the end of the company's first day on the market, then double and double again. This time, investors sought out Villafana.

St. Jude Medical was launched in the summer of 1976 with private funds. Peter Gombrich, then executive vice president, remembers efforts to perfect the valve design. "For three or four months, we did nothing but brainstorm. We worked with all kinds of sketches and ideas, making models out of anything we could find—toilet-paper tubes, modeling clay. The problem was to insert the leaflets into the ring without breaking the ring. At one point, we thought we had it. Manny went out to talk to the investors, and then it broke. We had nothing but failures. Then one night I woke up with a dream about the valve. I got up and went to the lab at 4:30, and from then on, we made it work." The company went public in 1977—a bad year for the stock market—with two offerings, one in February, with stock selling at $3.50, and one in December, at $6.50 a share.

By October 1977, the company began selling its new valve. Within a year, St. Jude Medical was breaking even. By 1980, sales had climbed to $12 million, and the future seemed to offer steady growth—until St. Jude found itself face to face with the U.S. Food and Drug Administration.

At about the time St. Jude Medical was selling its first shares of stock, the FDA had received the power to regulate medical devices. Products that carried significant risk—such as heart valves—had to be clinically tested in limited numbers, the FDA declared. By 1980, the FDA had decided St. Jude had sold far too many valves. The agency sought to limit St. Jude's sales until information on the 15,000 implanted valves could be gathered and evaluated.

The FDA cost the company a year's time. It was a painful lesson and a costly mistake. "We just got off on the wrong foot," Villafana says. "The regulations came out just as we were getting started, so we didn't have much of an idea what the guidelines would be. When we finally saw them we realized that some of the blood samples had to be collected before the patient received the valve."

Painstaking retrieval finally produced data that satisfied the FDA, and by the end of 1981 approval seemed assured. Meanwhile, the company had grown to 110 employees— and the restless Manny Villafana was once again ready to move on.

Why would an entrepreneur go through the uncertainty of founding a company, garnering its share of the market, recruiting employees—and then leave, just as the enterprise began to look solidly successful?

For Manny Villafana, the answer lies within himself. His rewards, it seems, are found not in building an empire, but in doing the impossible. "I hate two expressions," he says. "One is 'It can't be done,' and the other is 'We've always done it this way.' At CPI, we were not the first to study the lithium-iodide battery. Pacemaker engineers in the big companies had looked at lithium and decided that pacemaker circuitry could not be made to use that kind of battery. Well, we didn't hire a single pacemaker engineer. We went to the computer industry for our engineers. They had no preconceived notions about what could or couldn't be done.

"When we decided to make the St. Jude valve out of carbon, people said it couldn't be done because carbon is too brittle. For a while, I was afraid they were right. I almost closed the doors of the company because I thought they might be right." But *he* believed that carbon was the best material for heart valves.

Villafana relied on the people he had chosen—one whose doctoral thesis had been in fluid dynamics, another who was "just a good gadgeteer." Eventually, the company made a carbon valve that didn't break. Villafana was right: it *could* be done.

☐ Villafana is quick to credit the contributions of others. An entrepreneur cannot be successful alone, he insists. "I think other people are the most important factor. Your mentor, if you have one. The people you ask for capital.

The specialists you need, the engineers, the marketing and financial people—the ability to bring in the people you need." And the most difficult aspect of starting a business is to convince those people it will succeed. "At first, you can offer no assurance that there will be a paycheck, that you will be able to raise the capital or even sell the idea," he says. "What can you offer people when you have no health insurance, pension plans or seniority? We all have a dream of doing our own thing. I promise people they will have a chance to do *their* own thing."

Then, as a company grows, he believes, the entrepreneur must relinquish authority and let others take over. "In the beginning, you wear a lot of different hats. You even scrub floors when they have to be scrubbed. Gradually, you give away the hats, one by one. You have to give up marketing and all the rest. Finally, you have only one hat left, and eventually you have to give that away, too." That hat, he says, is given away when the company is no longer an entrepreneurial effort, "when what is needed is day-to-day planning and cash flow and all those things. They all have their place—but not in the heart of an entrepreneur."

"You also have to remember that the people you bring in have their own goals. You can only have one president, one boss, and they would all like to take a crack at it. I have a theory that a president should step aside after five years. A company that is going to succeed needs fresh ideas and different skills."

Another critical factor, Villafana believes, is "faith in your own instincts." He says, "Often, in a large company, you never have to make the truly difficult decisions. Someone above you makes them. But when you're the entrepreneur, you're faced with *all* the decisions, and you have to have faith in your instincts."

Villafana's instincts told him to go 100 percent with lithium batteries at CPI—even when Wilson Greatbatch, the inventor, urged him to first make a more traditional pacemaker. "I told Greatbatch we were willing to take whatever he would give us," Villafana recalls. " 'But it won't last 10 years,' Greatbatch said. 'Fine, will it last three years?' I asked. 'That's twice as long as pacemakers last now.' Just to show you how wrong he was, the first lithium-powered pacemakers are nine years old, and they're still running."

Villafana also believes in sharing the financial risk. "If you form a company properly, there's no need to take the entire risk, making you or your family so apprehensive about loss that it affects your thinking. If you raise the capital from a multitude of people, they share the risk as well as the reward. Some people believe they have to retain at least 51 percent of the stock in order to keep control. But that's an illusion. If you're doing a good job, nobody will bother you. If you're not, you shouldn't be there."

Manny Villafana possesses, his colleagues say, the ability to see unexpected potential in others, to create a championship team with unlikely players. "He pulled the CPI team together and made them believe they could accomplish the impossible," says his attorney, Thomas Garrett III. "The same way he took a few people who didn't appear to be gifted and led them to create what might be the best heart valve in the world." Villafana believes that people who have been in an industry for a long time are less likely than newcomers to make important discoveries. Myopia, he calls it.

In part, Villafana's success stems from his ability to sell his ideas to employees, to investment bankers, to attorneys. Yet Villafana is less than comfortable with his reputation as a super-salesman. "People misinterpret my selling ability," he insists. "What I'm really doing is teaching. I don't care what it is that people are buying—something for the home, an air conditioner, an electric blanket—they like to learn how it works." In the early days of St. Jude Medical, Tom Garrett recalls, Villafana read volumes on heart valves, educating first himself, then his employees.

Villafana recognizes the toll of time and energy a start-up company exacts: "It takes 100 percent attention for five years." In his 40s now, he recognizes that his original incentives have evaporated. "I don't need to make a lot of money now, and I don't have to prove anything to anybody," he says. "Still, there are products that need to be made...."

Villafana is proud of his pacemakers and the St. Jude valve—and of their contributions to medicine. "During the early years at CPI, we were the leader in technology," he says. "I can list 10 things we did first that every pacemaker company does now. When we started St. Jude, everybody said we were entering a dying industry. Most defective valves were damaged by rheumatic fever, a declining illness in the United States. But I knew rheumatic fever was not eradicated in developing countries. There were other degenerative diseases that made heart valves harden and calcify. Also, surgeons were becoming more aggressive about replacing defective valves. I believed there was a market."

To many in the medical industry, Villafana is an enigma. His distaste for detail has come back to haunt him more than once. For instance, he "forgot" to pick up written release of the pacemaker project from Med General, grounds for one of the two lawsuits that plagued CPI in its early years. Yet his proposals to investment bankers are well-documented, and his budgets are complete to the last Telex. He is known as headstrong and tireless, yet he is proud that in 15 years no employee working directly for him has quit. He has difficulty firing anyone. He drives a hard bargain, yet he is extremely generous with his time and his wealth. Kips Bay Boys' Club has received contributions from Villafana that run into six figures. He also serves on its board of directors.

Villafana is strict, particularly with his children, yet he says he never holds a grudge. He thrives on international sales, yet doesn't like to travel. He collects classic cars and elaborate, antique clocks, but he's an extremely conservative investor. In July 1981, he threw a party for 280 friends, yet the 10 years of "100 percent attention" have left him, he says, with very few who are close.

There have been other costs, too. Not enough time for his family. Strained relationships. A nine-month separation. Difficulty in differentiating between home and business roles. "An entrepreneur has a real problem," he concedes. "At work, he's the boss—no question. At home, he doesn't have the same authority, and it's hard to make the transition."

Villafana's health has also suffered with his unyielding attention to business. "Three years ago, I felt like a 99-year-old man," he says. "Not only was I physically out of shape, but I was narrow. I could talk about little else except medical devices and my industry. So I expanded my sights, took up racquetball, downhill skiing. I even volunteered for a broomball tournament!"

Even so, there is little in Manny Villafana's life that he

would have changed. He encourages would-be entrepreneurs to take the plunge. "Most people are afraid to try. I say, if you don't, it will always eat at you. If you have enough in the bank to live on, give yourself a year. If it hasn't worked in nine months, take the last three to look for a job. At least you tried."

He offers five tenets as a guide in the long search for financial backing. "The first is honesty—be frank about what you're going to do and what your chances are. Second, don't be afraid to ask for a large amount—going back for money a second time can be brutal. Third, teach —educate people technically. Fourth, have the very best people you can get on your team, and emphasize their strengths. They are your vote of confidence. Last, don't make wild projections."

☐ Not long ago, Manny Villafana came upon a Superman pin that caught his eye. He had it encased in acrylic, along with two favorite axioms. "If you have tried to do something and failed, you are vastly better off than if you had tried to do nothing and succeeded." And: "The great pleasure in life is doing what people say you cannot do."

He presented that Superman "trophy" to an entrepreneur who had just given a year to starting a new company.

Earl Olson

10

Earl Olson

Betting on the Bird

Earl Olson had horse-trader in his blood, thanks to his father. He also inherited the gumption to get up and leave.

Small-scale farming on the parched western Minnesota plains near Murdock bore only a subsistence living for Olaf Olson, his wife and two sons. Even at 13, Earl Olson knew he wanted more than 25 milk cows and 160 acres yielding meager corn and soybean crops year after year. That farm had been the gold ring for Olaf, a Swedish immigrant, who scraped together his down payment by selling ponies to the American horse brigade. But it was no place for his ambitious son, who was spoonfed on both the Protestant work ethic and the American dream.

Young Earl Olson knew all about hard work. He was up at 5 a.m. daily to milk the half-dozen Holsteins assigned to him. He repeated the chore at dusk. It was the same routine Sundays and holidays with no exceptions. He'd been following that routine since he was six. He knew those cows were the family profit center. Without milk money during the Depression, his father would have lost the farm.

So Earl pitched in. The boy learned about vicious cycles—oversupply dragging commodity prices to the dregs; undersupply pushing them upward again, only to spawn a dangerous optimism. Bad weather buffeted crops. Streaks of ugly luck were interrupted by just enough good fortune to risk another season. Farming Minnesota's flatlands during the 1920s was living on the edge.

So Earl Olson up and left Murdock when he was 13. Somehow, for this callow prairie youth, the risk of leaving home was less fearsome than the risk of staying too long. The boy's father understood—37 years earlier, at 19, Olaf Olson had left Sweden for America. He, too, had been alone.

Earl Olson headed 40 miles west to Morris where he enrolled in the West Central School of Agriculture. He found a room and earned most of his tuition shoveling coal or unloading lumber from railroad cars at 12 cents an hour.

As it happened, his first step away from Murdock was only the first of many. Today, Earl Olson owns at least 28 turkey farms, together more than 300 times the size of his father's original 160-acre spread. His company, Jennie-O Foods, based in Willmar, is the largest privately held producer of turkeys and turkey products in the world, growing three-million birds and processing at least eight million annually. His company generates more than $100 million in sales a year, and Olson owns virtually all of it.

Credit a young man's prairie gumption and a horse-trader's eye for opportunity for much of that amazing journey.

□ The first step, ironically, was back in the direction from which he had come. Fresh out of agricultural school in the spring of 1932, Earl Olson, then 17, landed a job as butter-maker's helper at the Murdock Cooperative Creamery. Olson's father, a creamery board member, helped put him on the path of this $34-a-month opportunity. And an opportunity it was, to be sure. Olson's boss spent more time closing the local bar than burning midnight oil so, by default, Earl found himself more and more in charge. Someone had to test the cream, churn the butter, fuel the creamery boiler and keep records. The manager had abdicated. For his efforts, the creamery board raised Olson's salary to $37.50.

When the chance came a year later to more than double his pay at another creamery, Olson grabbed it. What did it matter if the destination was a near-bankrupt enterprise? The cooperative board at Swift Falls Creamery, 20 miles away, offered a carrot—$100 a month plus one percent of all sales. Olson liked the challenge. If he could keep Swift Falls from being yet another victim of the Depression, he would profit handily.

The answer was service. Traditionally, the farmers around Swift Falls drove 15, 20 or 30 miles round-trip every other day to sell their milk and eggs to the creamery. Most everybody did it, but farmers resented the time they spent in transit. "Why not go to them?" Olson asked his board. Why not beat the competition by saving the farmers a trip. But Olson's conservative board would not spend money on a delivery truck.

Unwilling to abandon that strategy, the 20-year-old creamery manager traded in his 1935 Chevrolet and borrowed $1,000 toward a $1,200 three-quarter-ton pick-up truck. He convinced Russell Hanson, the Swift Falls banker, to back him. Before it was due, Olson paid back the $1,000 loan, impressing Hanson and paving the way for future business loans.

Mornings at 4, Olson rolled out of bed, climbed into his truck and made his rounds of the western Minnesota countryside, picking up eggs and milk. Before long, he bought a second truck, hired a driver, and created three pick-up routes that occupied the driver full-time. The strategy worked, and, all the while, Olson's salary was growing.

The roving creamery fleet then grew to three trucks and two drivers. To make those trips even more profitable, Olson started offering livestock feed and seed corn to his farming customers. Before long, the Swift Falls Creamery also bought poultry, turkeys and other livestock. The truck routes grew almost weekly as a parade of commodities from the country poured into Olson's burgeoning enterprise. Olson returned the favor with an expanded line of supplies from the creamery—seed, feed, fertilizer, shovels, hoes, tack, even ice cream.

All those sidelines gave Olson the competitive edge—what the Swift Falls Creamery made on sideline sales offset the sweetened price Olson offered farmers for their eggs and milk. No one in the region could afford to pay more for produce than Olson, and the farmers flocked to him. Suppliers became spenders; spenders became suppliers. The momentum seemed irreversible, and other cooperative managers saw red. What was once a near-bankrupt creamery had become a powerhouse. While other cooperators had no cause to cry foul, they could—and did—loudly criticize the upstart Olson for carrying competition miles beyond the rural comfort level.

At 23, Olson was riding high. He was making money for the creamery and himself. Competition aroused him, and he was eager to better his own sales records. The only element that bothered Olson was a fiercely conservative board of directors. Let it go for now, he thought—they won't meddle with success.

Then one day in 1938, a woman walked into the Swift Falls Creamery to buy ice. Olson was moving, typically, at top speed—weighing cream, testing it for butterfat content, selling feed, jotting figures in his ledger. "A dime's worth?" he said. "Right away, ma'am." He always emphasized service at the creamery, even on picayune purchases like ice. He rushed into the freezer, chopped off a dime-size hunk, pushed open the heavy, insulated door and headed back to the counter. But there was a collision. Milo Ellingson, Olson's only on-site helper at the creamery, was moving a thousand gallons of scalding-hot water toward the freezer door just as Olson emerged with the ice. The water momentarily paralyzed Olson. It scalded his legs and feet. The pain surpassed description.

"Patch up my legs," he told a doctor in the local hospital emergency room. "I have to be back to work in the morning."

"I'm sorry," the doctor answered, "you'll be with us a while." When he removed Olson's shoes and socks, the skin went with them. Those were serious burns—enough to hospitalize Olson for three months.

Lying in his hospital bed, his legs caked with tar to enhance healing, Olson had plenty of time to think. He was immobile, away from the controls, upset because he believed the creamery could not function without him. He was not one to delegate easily. Nor would he abdicate authority just because the burns had put him on his back.

Olson reached for the telephone and stayed on it day

after day, calling customers to encourage their continued business and managing the creamery at a distance. Reluctantly, he learned to delegate—but only to expedite business. His employees knew it. The creamery board, seeing Olson's resolve, voted to continue his salary and let him collect his one percent commission during the entire hospital stay.

If the telephone was Olson's umbilical cord to the creamery he nurtured, his hospital room was a womb for the germination of ideas. Captive as he was, Olson thought and schemed. This setback would not impede him; he would leverage the $1,000 in accident insurance money he received because of the accident. A single man with no dependents or financial responsibilities, he found it hard to remember why he bought that policy in the first place. No matter. He'd purchased the insurance, and now it would work for him.

Turkeys, Olson decided. Olson would use his $1,000 to buy 300 young turkeys from a hatchery, feed and medication from his own creamery and a hired hand to help raise the birds. Turkeys would be Olson's personal business. The market was ready for more turkeys. He knew that supply trailed demand. He would sell his flock to the Swift Falls Creamery, and the creamery would resell the birds at a profit. Swift Falls would benefit from more poultry business, and Olson would profit twice—first as a supplier to the creamery, then as creamery manager with a one-percent cut of total sales. It was a tidy thought. Equally important, Olson would have a venture of his own.

☐ Earl Olson raised those turkeys in an outdoor pen near his home in Swift Falls. He bought each day-old bird for 30 cents and tended the flock on weekends. Folks in Swift Falls, especially Olson's neighbors, shook their heads and wondered. Surely he was destined to go broke with this venture. It would serve him right, too, the neighbors muttered. Damn turkeys wouldn't stay put—they took to nearby roofs and left droppings in yards and on sidewalks. Couldn't Olson simply stick to business at the creamery and leave it at that?

Hardly. In that first year, 1941, Olson made $1 a bird on his 300 turkeys. It was enough to make him triple his flock the next year. Again, Olson enjoyed $1 profit per bird. The following year, 1943, Olson boosted his flock to 5,000, believing in a logical profit progression. The more turkeys he raised, the more $1-per-head gains he made. It was simple arithmetic.

Five-thousand dollars of profit on a single flock was a seductive figure next to his monthly salary at the Swift Falls Creamery. And the return on investment seduced him. By 1948, Olson, the part-time turkey grower, had expanded his flock to 12,000 birds. It was a particularly good year, and Olson's profits skyrocketed to $4 a bird. The Swift Falls Creamery had established one of the few turkey-processing plants in the five-state area, and, before long, Olson would be producing more turkeys than the plant could process. Not only that, the creamery now employed 100 people—25 more than the total population of Swift Falls. Turkeys had everything to do with this new-found prosperity.

That did it. Olson forgot about commodity cycles. He was enticed by profit and the prospect of turning a backyard enterprise into a full-fledged business—his own.

□ Olson ordered 35,000 day-old turkeys in 1949. He competed strenuously with other turkey growers enticed by the same profits in a market where demand still exceeded supply. Olson saw his order trimmed by 5,000 birds—he could secure no more—and he raised 30,000 that year. The cutback, it turned out, was a minor blessing.

That year, Olson lost almost $2 a bird, or a total of nearly $60,000. The sum was 50 times his annual salary at the creamery.

Olson was shocked. He thought back to his early years on the 160-acre farm, the unflappable optimism in Olaf Olson's fibre and the inevitable cycles. The $60,000 bath, he decided, was part of a cycle. The turkey market, he reasoned, was still sound, and resilient growers with an eye on the long haul would survive and prosper. He simply had to remember and anticipate the cycles. He had to remember his past.

Olson learned another important lesson during that period: Manage from a distance only if you can bank on the help. The creamery in Marietta, Minnesota, looked like a promising venture for Olson and his colleague from near-by Cyrus, Gilbert Ahlstrand. The business was producing a

million pounds of butter annually and ringing up about
$500,000 in sales. The price was right, too—Olson and
Ahlstrand put up just $15,000 apiece. But the creamery
was no bargain without a good, full-time manager, and
the partners went through a string of them. None demonstrated the entrepreneurship Olson felt when he first went
to work at Swift Falls.

Olson managed to visit Marietta and look at the operation first-hand only four times a year. Ahlstrand made it
once a month. The pair were absentee managers, and their
distance soon showed. More competitive creameries
eclipsed Marietta, and the venture merely broke even. If
Olson could be ambivalent about a business enterprise, it
was this one. "It didn't make any money," Olson told a
colleague years later, "so it wasn't interesting." He
discovered he could not replicate the Swift Falls experience
at a distance. He would not keep his distance again.

By 1949, the Swift Falls Creamery's turkey-processing
business was healthy and growing. In fact, there were more
turkeys to process than Swift Falls could handle. Olson
saw an opportunity in All State Supply of Willmar. The
company wanted to sell its unprofitable turkey-processing
plant, and Olson encouraged his board to buy it. But the
board said no. It would require a change in the cooperative
bylaws, the board members said. But more than administrative alterations, the board resisted long-term debt. They
were status-quo thinkers. To Olson, maintaining the status
quo meant that the creamery would slip slowly and steadily
behind.

Although he'd lost $60,000 on his own turkey operation,
Olson decided to risk more. *He* would buy the Willmar
processing plant—for $100,000—and lease it to the Swift
Falls Creamery. The Swift Falls board, in turn, would pay
a cent per pound of processed turkey, plus all expenses
associated with keeping Olson's plant running, at least for
one year. "If I could build the Swift Falls Creamery up
from nothing," Olson thought, "I can do the same with
All State's processing plant." Olson also knew that once a
country co-op makes a financial comeback, its board is not
above hiring a cut-rate manager to carry on. He had seen it
happen before, and he decided he would not be a victim of
that cost-cutting mentality.

Olson's financing, meanwhile, was not to come from

Russell Hanson at the Swift County Bank. Hanson thought the 33-year-old entrepreneur was a good bet, but Hanson's loan limit was only $15,000. Olson left the bank deflated. But minutes later, Hanson had another idea and loped up behind Olson on Main Street. "This is a long shot," Hanson told him, "but if you'll pick me up at 6 a.m. tomorrow morning, we'll drive to Minneapolis and talk to the officers at Midland National Bank."

It was a spit-and-polished Earl Olson who turned up in the carpeted sanctum of a big-city bank the next day. Hanson introduced his young friend to the loan committee, saying: "He's just a kid. He has little money. But he has good experience, he's honest, and he always pays his bills." The loan committee dispatched Olson to the anteroom. Twenty minutes later, they called him back and told him he had $75,000 at five percent, payable over a decade. Olson would seek financing many times over the next 30 years. He learned to sell bankers with the same zeal he sold turkey growers on his young operation. And he would learn about "creative financing" years before the phrase became a common part of a businessman's vocabulary.

Olson's new turkey-processing plant earned $40,000 on four-million pounds of turkey during his first full year of operation. Olson was also drawing his $1,200-a-year salary from the Swift Falls Creamery, $26,000 in annual commission fees, plus income from a fleet of trucks hauling turkeys for the creamery. At 35, Olson was earning more than twice the salary of the governor of Minnesota. The notion enchanted him. But Olson was also heavily leveraged—a condition he would have to accept for a lifetime in the volatile turkey business. However, each risk, measured against the growth that came from it, encouraged him. When it came time to sever his relationship with the Swift Falls Creamery for good, Olson was ready.

Another business disagreement was the catalyst. Turkey growers were strapped for cash after prices plummeted in 1949. No longer would they sell their turkeys on consignment to the Swift Falls Creamery. Cash on delivery—that was the new stipulation—but the creamery board wouldn't go along with it. We have to come up with the cash, Olson argued, or lose the growers' business. He and the board were at loggerheads. Olson believed the only choice he had was to finance the growers himself. It meant another trip to the bank, more commitment and more risk. But he would do it and leave the creamery behind him.

Within two years after Olson left Swift Falls, the creamery he'd brought back to life a decade earlier went bankrupt. When he left, he'd taken the turkey-processing and marketing business with him. By 1950, that business accounted for approximately 75 percent of all creamery revenues. Yet he could not feel responsible for the creamery's demise. The board had had its chance. Now Olson was a competitor. Furthermore, he was determined to be a dominant force in the marketplace. The prospect of a poor Murdock farm kid taking on the likes of Armour, Land O'Lakes and Swift lured him. It was an enticing David-and-Goliath scenario.

□ Olson set about gaining the confidence of Minnesota turkey growers. The soft-spoken Swede was convincing. After all, he was one of them. He had grown up in western Minnesota, raised turkeys in his own back yard and learned early how to dress birds. Olson was just plain folks, a good salesman, a canny negotiator. Growers knew that Olson understood them. Most important, when he needed to clinch a deal, Olson could offer one-half to two cents more per pound than any other buyer in the region. Olson had cultivated the Eastern markets. He no longer needed distributors and brokers; he could sell direct. Olson's western Minnesota competitors couldn't match his price.

Olson worked 18-hour days making the rounds of the growers. Occasionally his oldest son, Charles, accompanied him. "Dad was in the midst of a bidding war," Charles recalls. "It was often a seller's market, with many processors clamoring for the same product. Deals were made verbally and were subject to change at a moment's notice. With luck, Dad had the last opportunity to up his bid to meet a competitor's. But who could be sure the other bid was real? Dad was never really sure he owned any turkeys until they were hanging on shackles in his plant. He always risked coming up short.

"The early 1950s took their toll," Charles Olson continues. "Dad was working hard and trying to survive. He had six people to support. That's when the ulcer developed.

I remember him being so sick on a trip to see growers, he asked me to drive him back to Willmar. I was 12." The ulcer was not enough, however, to make Earl Olson cut back on his work load. Nothing—not even his family—could do that.

"Earl had incredible stamina," Ted Huisinga, of Willmar Poultry and Egg Company, a competitor and ally, observes. "I saw turkey growers cuss him out, get mad as hell about price or grade, but Earl, that stubborn Swede, would still be back buying their next flock. He was truly a diplomat. Earl had an ability to treat unfriendly growers as friends."

If Olson was to succeed, he needed a consistent supply of turkeys, even if that meant paying growers cash on delivery. By 1952, Olson was processing approximately $100,000 worth of turkeys daily. But wide fluctuations in the market made growers unwilling to wait for Olson to process their birds and sell them before they saw their dollars. "After our trucks loaded up their turkeys and headed back to the Willmar plant," Olson remembers, "those growers followed immediately, expecting payment on the spot. I thought, 'If they'd only wait 10 days for their checks, at $100,000 a day that would amount to $1 million of free credit.' "

The growers, Olson surmised, needed a shot of confidence. So at a time when he was least able to afford it, he bought the fanciest Cadillac Fleetwood he could find. He considered the car his "public relations project on wheels." He reasoned that if growers saw him roving the back roads of western Minnesota in *that* prize, they would assume he was successful—so successful they could be assured of payment for their turkeys. The image-builder worked (and Olson learned to savor his new-found elegance). One by one, the growers told Olson he could mail their checks after processing was complete.

At the same time, Olson raised his own turkeys for processing on the Earl B. Olson Farms. He learned early the value of vertical integration. All through the 1950s, most live turkeys were processed and sold from October through January. If Olson could raise and process his own turkeys when outside growers weren't producing, he could develop a year-round business and keep his plants busy continuously. He knew that the more roles he could play between egg and table, the more money he would make and the more control he would have. Control was a familiar idea to Earl Olson—he had been looking for ways to control his destiny since he left the family farm at 13.

With his year-round production plan, Olson had to convince buyers that turkey was more than a holiday entree. It would take years, but Olson would succeed by selling more products than whole frozen turkeys wrapped in plastic. Olson would "further process" his turkeys and turn those whole birds into turkey loaves, turkey ham, turkey wieners, and tidy little packages containing drumsticks, breasts, thighs and wings. Before long, Olson—in his effort to use every part of the feathered creatures—would even package turkey tails and sell them to soup-cooks in the Orient.

Why not? Olson was out to capture a market wherever he found it. When the Army asked him, in 1955, if he could produce a boneless turkey for shipment to overseas bases, he quickly obliged. Images of multimillion-dollar contracts danced in Olson's head, and he became the first turkey supplier to the armed forces. Acceptance by the government gave Olson the knowledge and impetus he needed to "go public" with his boneless turkey roast in retail markets.

Olson then sought a brand name. While Earl Olson's Farmer's Produce Company served him well in the beginning—it conjured up an image of wholesome, country cooperation—it was not very snappy. New York retailers urged him to develop a name consumers could ask for at the meat counter. "Jennie-O," Olson's wife suggested over Thanksgiving dinner in 1956. "Jennie" was the name of their only daughter; "O" was, of course, for Olson. "Hell of a name," an important distributor told Olson the next day. "Short and snappy. Change your company name and market your turkeys under the Jennie-O brand." He did. It's been Jennie-O Foods ever since.

☐ Julius Davis, of the Minneapolis law firm Robins, Davis & Lyons, was a key advisor to Olson at the time. All along, Olson had an eye for acquisitions. "He smelled them," one of Olson's bankers recalls, "and Julie Davis figured out how to get them. Julie was great with figures and an ace negotiator." Olson spotted his acquisition targets easily. He could see competitors falter as he sliced off pieces of their business.

Litchfield Produce was just such a target in 1957. For years, the Litchfield operation had threatened Olson. It was easily four times larger than Olson's enterprise, it was located just a few miles away from him, and it competed vigorously for the same turkey growers. Over time, however, Olson's sweetened prices to growers and his greater control over costs had helped eclipse the Litchfield operation. Not only that, Olson had specialized in turkeys while Litchfield Produce appeared to dilute its efforts with chickens and eggs.

Litchfield Produce was near bankruptcy when the bidding war began between Olson's Jennie-O Foods and Armour & Company. Olson was not one to back away because Armour was formidable by its very size. Through the grapevine, Olson and Julius Davis learned that Armour was offering $100,000 for the Litchfield facility. "That was legal stealing," Olson says. "The plant was actually worth close to $1 million." Furthermore, Olson needed it —his Willmar processing plant had reached capacity. If Jennie-O's growth was to continue uninterrupted, the company needed new production quickly.

One Friday afternoon, while Armour employees were already moving packing boxes and supplies into their soon-to-be-acquired Litchfield plant, Olson and Davis nailed down a $108,000 offer. "That's our first and final offer," Olson told the Litchfield owners. "It must be accepted by Monday at 8 a.m., or we'll withdraw the bid and make no others." Olson and Davis banked on Armour's size: The meat-packing giant could not assemble its board and respond in a single weekend. They were right. By Monday, Jennie-O Foods had a new plant that raised Earl Olson's annual production in 1959 to two-million turkeys. The empire-building had begun.

Other acquisitions followed in rapid succession. Melrose Produce Company was another victim of the volatile turkey market. In less than a week, Olson bought the Melrose firm for "a penny down and 10 years to pay." That 1960 acquisition increased Olson's production by another million turkeys. In 1963, Olson bought a Swift Falls feed mill, in 1965 a Willmar elevator and in 1966 a Brainerd feed mill.

It was not an easy time for acquisitions, but Olson the opportunist made his strategy work. Many turkey growers and processors were the victims of their own optimism and overproduction in the 1960s. Violent swings in turkey prices all but destroyed Olson's finances. In 1967 alone he lost nearly $1 per bird on one-million turkeys, and he suffered additional financial setbacks in his processing business.

"People in western Minnesota looked at Earl Olson with a feeling of awe," a close friend and turkey grower, Lloyd Peterson, remembers. "They shook their heads and wondered if he could survive. Earl was always operating on the edge financially. When he sold $300,000 worth of debentures in 1961 at seven percent and guaranteed his investors a double return in 10 years, people thought Earl had gone crazy. But it was his way of raising some of the additional capital he needed without selling the store. He would not give up that control. Earl relied on his guts and determination during the 1960s. All the while, he seemed to be going about his business calmly when, in fact, he held a mountain of tension inside."

Olson went back to his bankers again and again. He sold his program hard, and his ambitious advocacy turned some people off. The turkey business was a terrific gamble, they thought, even for the most savvy entrepreneur. Over time, however, the Twin Cities banking establishment found Olson surprisingly accurate with his forecasts and honest about his intentions. Olson, they learned, was a straight-shooter—he leveled early with the bankers when his business turned bad.

And turn bad it did in 1962. But the cause wasn't a poor turkey market, it was an ill-fated chicken venture with the Peavey Company of Minneapolis, Jack Frost Hatcheries of St. Cloud and All State Hatcheries of Willmar. Peavey, a major Upper Midwest feed dealer, was interested in a joint venture to grow, process and market broiler chickens in Minnesota. To ensure consistent supply, Jennie-O, Peavey and the other two partners agreed to pay no less than 18 cents per pound for broilers, regardless of the market. Then the market dropped to 10 cents a pound. Northern transportation costs also far exceeded those for competing chicken producers in Southern states. In addition, Olson and his partners were novices in the chicken trade. Olson and Jennie-O lost half-a-million dollars over three years on that venture. "Earl has always been a plunger," a friend explains. "Nothing ventured, nothing gained."

But Olson had learned to live with cycles. His answer to failure was to take personal responsibility and turn the situation around. There would be no buckling to outside forces, no blaming others. Olson busied himself convincing his chicken suppliers to convert their operations to turkey production. When he finished his pitch, he had persuaded 30 growers in west-central Minnesota to make the conversion. The new contingent hiked Jennie-O's production by approximately 25 percent and gave Olson the additional cash he needed to support his acquisitive instincts.

Olson took other flyers, too. After the market downturn of 1967, he reasoned that many turkey growers would be so disheartened by their losses, they would cut production or quit the business altogether. Banking on that, he expanded his production by half-a-million birds for the 1968 season. Undersupply boosted turkey prices from about 40 cents a pound in 1967 to 60 cents in 1968, and Olson profited handily. He had learned to gamble and win. Over 30 years in business, he had fine-tuned his instincts for risk and reward.

If he was to continue to succeed in that fashion, Olson believed he could not give up his authoritarian control of Jennie-O Foods. The company would remain forever closely held, unencumbered by too many outside voices and capable of swift action. Only once, in fact, did Olson sell a portion of his company. He sold 50 percent to Peavey when he needed capital after the chicken debacle. Even so, the shared ownership didn't last long. Twenty-four months later, Olson bought the 50 percent back. Fortunately, for Olson, the turkey market took a dive about that time, and Peavey sold at a bargain price.

"I wanted to own my own business," Olson says today. "I didn't want stockholders, committee meetings and countless consultations. I wanted to move faster than those elements would allow. I wanted to make decisions at the snap of my fingers. My Swift Falls Creamery experience reinforced that need."

Today's Jennie-O Foods has a board of directors with two outsiders and two insiders—Earl Olson and his son

Charles, now company president. Two other Olson off-spring, Bruce and Jeff, also work in Jennie-O manage-ment.

Earl Olson has always expected to pass the torch to his eldest son. There was no question that the patriarch chose to ensure leadership within the family. It was an important legacy. "In those early years, our business was too risky to appeal to investors," he says, "but, later on, people wanted to buy in. We never wanted to sell. We wanted to keep our business in the family."

As long as he remains in Jennie-O's corporate offices on Highway 12 in Willmar, Earl Olson will be the ultimate boss. "I would hate to serve on the Jennie-O board," a long-time observer says, "and be on the other side of Earl Olson. He is still very much a presence. Earl is accustomed to running things his way."

☐ Earl Olson, who frequently uses the term "we" when he really means "I," is not shy about his need for achieve-ment. "I think we always wanted to be the largest in-dependently owned turkey processor in the world," he says. "We thought we could do it. We were determined. Friends in similar businesses just quit too soon. We were willing to work hard, persevere, ride through the down cycles. We always thought there was a way to overcome the negatives.

"My parents lived a truly meager life. I think about my father working a lifetime to pay for one 160-acre farm. Now we're able to buy a farm many times that size and pay for it in a few months." When Olson makes that com-parison, he seems alternately amazed and pleased. More than earnings, power and position are important to him.

Charles, the heir apparent, reminds Earl of himself—soft-spoken, stoical, resourceful. Charles has been the most energetic advocate of "further processing," a strategy that has expanded the Jennie-O line to some 100 different turkey products. Charles is gradually taking con-trol of the family enterprise, although he admits that his father, now 67, has difficulty with even subtle shifts in authority.

Father and son have offices within 15 feet of one another in Jennie-O's modest headquarters. The walls of Earl Olson's office are loaded with honorary degrees, citations for business achievement and congenial photos of himself with Republican politicians. Prominent on Charles' office wall is a photo montage of his grandfather Olaf Olson—Swedish immigrant, horse-trader and small farmer—who died recently at age 98.

"Too tough to die young," folks in Murdock said of the old man. "Out working in his own field on his 95th birthday. Wouldn't even take a break to cut the cake because there was more to be done before dark."

The legacy represented in those photos has not been wasted.

Dean Scheff

11

Dean Scheff

A Jury of One

As a boy he was sickly, given to night-long asthma attacks and perpetual skin rash. He seemed to play host to every germ traveling through rural southwestern Minnesota. He missed weeks of school in the first grade, so much in fact that he was slow to learn to read. His mother worried that young Dean would be, in her words, "backward."

But the puny kid who was plagued by illnesses and who learned to read late became the founder of a $100-million company that makes its business in words—word-processing, the high-technology answer to typing words on paper. It is a process enhanced by high-speed printers, display screens and microcomputers that not only store words and ideas but sort them, massage them and retrieve them—all at the touch of a typewriter key.

The company is CPT Corporation of Eden Prairie, Minnesota, and the adult Dean Scheff is no weakling. He has wrestled business from the likes of IBM and Xerox. He has fortified his corporation's bottom line during years when older and presumably wiser competitors sacrificed themselves to red ink. He has ruled CPT with managerial muscle.

Critics call him a dictator or worse. And to that charge the combative Dean Scheff responds with a verbal smash down the center line. "Flakes," he calls them. Critics indeed play supporting roles to Dean Scheff's personal resolve. *They* did not start and build CPT Corporation—*he* did. They are but spectators, "flakes," nothing more. The sickly boy turned corporate strongman is very definitely in control.

□ Dean Scheff's singular style was developed early. The second child born to Fred and Malinda Scheff in August 1931 was a loner. His father ran a grain elevator in Wirock and, later, Lime Creek, Minnesota, but young Dean could have no part of that business because of his asthma. Dean had few friends his own age. All eight grades of school-age children in the country around Wirock and Lime Creek scarcely filled a single room.

Dean's answer to that childhood isolation was reading, even though he had a "lazy eye" that would not keep pace with the other. He missed a lot of school, but the kid was determined. Once he did learn how to read, he devoured histories and biographies, electronics texts and science fiction. He also developed into a fair high school football player, small but nimble. And he understood the profit motive. At six years of age, he was selling garden seed, Christmas cards and "magic" salve door to door. He sent in coupons cut out of comic books to put himself in business, but his market, alas, was limited. Even if the folks in Lime Creek and Wirock liked his pitch, he had, at best, only 30 potential customers.

Scheff's father taught him something of risk-taking—along with owning a country elevator, Fred Scheff dabbled in commodities futures. "I can recall times when he came home walking one foot off the ground because some commodity went up three cents," Dean Scheff says. "And I remember him lower than a snake's bellybutton when things went down four cents. If he owned 100,000 of anything—which he did at times—that would be a $4,000 loss."

But Fred Scheff had blind spots when it came to risk, his son says. "After World War II, the government was stockpiling grain in bins around the country," Dean says. "Some farmers became phenomenally wealthy selling their grain to the government. But my father was so anti-government, he didn't take advantage of the opportunity. It was virtually no-risk. He should have taken it."

There were others, too, who set entrepreneurial examples for the boy. Two eager, scheming uncles collected ventures the way some men collect barroom jokes. They repeatedly borrowed money from Scheff's father to finance yet another "deal of a lifetime" and often lost the stake quickly. "At least they didn't make 'venture' a dirty word in my vocabulary," Dean says today. "No, I looked at my uncles—one in particular—and thought that if he could be successful over the long haul, anybody could...."

As it happened, Scheff took two detours before he entered the business world. The man who later turned out to be a tough, autocratic corporate chairman first enrolled in a pre-seminary major at Concordia College. By his third year, however, he balked. "My mother and my minister ganged up on me and absolutely twisted my arm," he says. "*They* decided I should be a minister. *I* decided enough of this! I rebelled and joined the Air Force."

Scheff was assigned to a troop ship among 2,800 enlisted men and 200 officers. The experience strengthened an early resolve to rise above the pack. "The officers bunked in the top part of the boat, the enlisted men in the bottom," he explains. "We were so far below the water level we would have had to climb upstairs to jump ship if a torpedo hit. Then and there I decided: Never again would I ride in the bottom of the boat."

☐ Later, with four years of service behind him, Scheff enrolled as an economics major at the University of Minnesota. He graduated during a recessionary slump (in 1957) when all the textbook economics he had learned paled beside the rising unemployment and tight money. He did have one job offer, from General Mills, but quickly scotched his chances with impertinence. "General Mills wanted a salesman, but sales was far from my mind," he says. "I thought it was demeaning work. Besides, my selling career ended when I was nine years old."

"If there's anything I don't want to do," Scheff announced during the job interview, "it's sell Wheaties...."

The interview ended quickly, and Scheff retreated to graduate school.

The young man's mouth got him in trouble again, however, when he eventually went before the board that would rule on his master's degree in business. In a setting where the master's candidate is always polite to his senior examiners, Scheff said flat-out that he disagreed with them. "My emphasis was industrial relations," he says. "At that time, the university was high on psychological testing for recruiting and hiring. I told them I believed the IQ test could be skewed—and they went bananas. They never did grant my master's degree."

It was not long afterward that Scheff, the industrial relations specialist without an advanced degree, discovered that he was virtually "unemployable." Too independent, too outspoken, too single-minded; resists regimentation, ignores chains of command, trusts almost no one. In his youth, a discipline problem; in adulthood, a maverick.

Scheff finally went to work for UNIVAC in St. Paul. His job was to find and train field service workers for the computer division of Sperry Rand, but dissatisfaction cut the assignment short. "I worked out of UNIVAC sales offices and discovered that the only thing salesmen do is sit around, look intelligent, drink coffee, wait for the phone to ring and pull in $20,000 a year," he says with typical hyperbole. "That was a lot more than I made in personnel." What's more, he says, "at one time, UNIVAC was synonymous with computers, but UNIVAC was losing out to IBM by the late 1950s, and I didn't want to work for a loser."

Scheff put aside his bias against selling and went in search of a new job. A New Jersey office-products firm needed sales representatives in Chicago. Scheff, his pregnant wife and the family dog headed for Chicago, pulling their belongings behind in a U-Haul trailer. Scheff visited his new office and, in casual conversation, asked about the strongest competition. "Friden, out of Minneapolis," he was told. "They're really tough."

Scheff thought about that information. "If they're so tough, why not join them?" he reasoned. "Then," he says, "I saw a sign that said, 'Minneapolis, 390 miles'." He parked the U-Haul and called his employer from a bar.

"I quit," Scheff said.

"But you haven't even *started*," the man answered.

"I don't like Chicago any more than I like New York."

"This whole thing is highly irregular," the man protested.

"So be it," said Scheff.

Scheff, his wife, the dog and the U-Haul headed north. And, upon arrival, Scheff knew precisely what to say when Friden's Minneapolis manager asked him why he wanted to work for the company. "I want to make money, plain and simple," Scheff replied. He was hired on the spot.

He was *not* a natural salesman. He pulled in about $300 a month at first. By that time, Dean and Diana Scheff had twin infants as well as themselves to feed. "I was no silver-tongued salesman," he says, "and it was tough getting people interested in the Friden Flexowriter. It was a complicated machine, threatening to many people. My basic ally was information. I knew how to install the equipment, and I knew how to solve problems."

His other "ally" during those early years was dogged determination. "I just knocked on doors for two years... so many doors," he says. "Most sales reps fail because they don't keep trying." Indeed, it was during that time that Scheff's Law was formulated. "Nobody ever dies from over-work," the Law states. "Over-eating, over-smoking, over-drinking—yes. But *not* over-working."

At Friden, Scheff was a persistent salesman-technician who knew his subject cold. The Scheff "data base" was a special weapon applied to those of little faith.

□ Dean Scheff met Richard Eichhorn at Friden in 1959. Both were Flexowriter salesmen, and both believed in beating on doors. Then, in 1962, Eichhorn left Friden to join the computer division at Honeywell. "Six months later, Dean called me," Eichhorn says. " 'Do you think you can get me a job?' he said. He was fed up with Friden. It was poorly run, there was turmoil in change, and the product line was deteriorating rapidly, he told me."

Eichhorn and Scheff became a sales team at Honeywell in 1963. Rather than wait for inquiry calls, the two men beat it to the street. They canvassed the Twin Cities, calling on North American Life Insurance, Fingerhut, Gold Bond Stamp Company, Farmers Insurance, St. Paul Insurance, Gelco Corporation. "We went to them instead of waiting for them to call us," says Eichhorn. Their targets were usually caught off balance and disarmed. Eichhorn and Scheff sold the Honeywell H200 Series, a new product, to Gelco. The price tag was about $500,000, and for two young men accustomed to selling souped-up typewriters, this seemed to be the ultimate. It was, in fact, the first H200 sale for Honeywell worldwide.

The "Dick and Dean Show" clicked. Scheff and Eichhorn went out on calls together and performed for potential customers like a pair of savvy troupers. Scheff's strength was perception. He could read the customer quickly and well. He could respond to subtle shifts in attitude. He was a quick study of people and circumstances. The team stayed together about nine months before splitting.

"Dean wanted to be his own boss," says Eichhorn. "He had a chance to start a Dura [office-machine] franchise in the Twin Cities, and I wanted to stay at Honeywell."

"I got $30 added to my check for selling a computer worth several hundreds of thousands of dollars," Scheff recalls. "That was enough of that. I wanted the opportunity to make more money rather than be shackled by an antiquated commission structure."

Scheff's departure was not a surprise. A pattern had developed. UNIVAC—dissatisfaction. Friden—dissatisfaction. Honeywell—dissatisfaction. The pattern was laced with perceived opportunity at the next stop.

Dura, which was based in Detroit, made, among other things, convertible-top mechanisms for the auto industry. But when the auto industry took a dive, Dura did, too. The company diversified into electronic office machines, although, as Scheff puts it, "they didn't have the faintest idea of what they were doing or why...except that it was the wave of the future." Scheff became a Dura dealer at first. Then he sold about 80 Dura typewriters and decided to buy a franchise.

The Dura machine was an adaptation of an IBM Selectric typewriter designed to increase a typist's output, but it proved to be unreliable. Almost half of the 15 people Scheff hired to work for him were service technicians assigned to fix the delicate machines. Before long, Scheff and his employees were rebuilding them as they arrived from the Dura plant.

"We were delivering two units a month to Control Data, so we took all the good parts out of 15 machines and put them into two for Control Data," Scheff says. "We worked weekends to make our machines more acceptable and make Control Data a better client. In the time it took to make a Dura acceptable, we finally thought we might as well build our own."

Scheff may have been building better machines, but his bottom line was in need of repair. He was selling the typewriters all right, but his expenses were too high, especially for service work. He was losing money on his own enterprise, even though he was the second most successful Dura dealer in the United States. A steady draw at Honeywell was beginning to look better than it had some five years earlier.

In the autumn of 1970, Scheff and Eichhorn met for lunch in the Honeywell cafeteria. They discovered their mutual envy.

"Dean, you're your own boss, you're free to choose your own hours, you have 15 people working for you, your sales are strong," Eichhorn said. "I envy you."

"Yeah, and look at you," Scheff countered. "Nice office, impressive title, the security of a big company, a regular paycheck. Every time I add the people I need, I go deeper in the hole."

"The security of Honeywell looked pretty good to Dean," Eichhorn recalls. "Not that he would have traded it."

Scheff was not about to leave his own business, but he was determined to end his association with Dura. He pulled out a legal pad and started sketching a device that he and one of his employees, Jim Weinhold, had developed. It was an automatic typewriter that stored information on magnetic tape cassettes—not on conventional paper tapes that coiled up in heaps on the floor and tore apart. The device also had an electronic keyboard instead of the electromechanical keyboard basic to the IBM Selectric. That meant it had fewer parts, needed fewer mechanical adjustments, was easier to service and was more responsive to the typist's touch. It could quadruple a typist's output, said Scheff.

IBM's machines were too complicated for most people, Scheff told Eichhorn. They were loaded with unnecessary features. Scheff's competitive philosophy would be different: produce a *simple* machine at an attractive price.

IBM had pioneered magnetic tape-driven typewriters, but Scheff believed he could offer his new word processor at half the price of IBM's MT/ST, particularly because IBM set the market price. Critics said IBM's price per unit ($7,500 to $10,000) was artificially high so customers would choose rental contracts more lucrative to IBM instead. Scheff said he intended to sell *his* word processors for about $4,200 to $5,000. He had no plans to follow IBM's example and lease units. What young company could afford to carry the up-front manufacturing expense while living on modest monthly leasing payments alone?

☐ Scheff's legal-pad scribblings intrigued Eichhorn. And, in May 1971, less than eight months after that lunch meeting, CPT (Cassette Powered Typewriters) Corporation was formed by the two friends. They began operating out of a converted bingo parlor on the 4200 block of Bloomington Avenue in south Minneapolis. Scheff was president and owned roughly 64 percent of the stock. Eichhorn owned 14 percent. The balance was divided between Norman Flaaten, sales manager for Friden's Data Processing Division and a former IBM office-products salesman, and John MacLennan, vice president of Eugene A. Hickok & Associates, a local engineering firm. Robert O. Knutson, an attorney, also served on the CPT board, but held no stock. Scheff, Eichhorn, MacLennan, Flaaten and Bill Head, a fifth investor, raised $140,000 in working capital for the new company.

"Dean definitely wanted to be boss," Eichhorn says. "The company was his idea, and he put in a significant amount of the start-up money."

"Dean looked at IBM and said, 'There must be a better way,'" says Marvin Geisness of Piper, Jaffray & Hopwood. "He knew there was because he was working with customers as a dealer every day. He knew their problems and needs intimately. He knew all about the competitive products available. He could look ahead. Dean is precognitive. He wasn't afraid of IBM. He believed he could develop a company and a product and compete with IBM head-on."

"I started CPT because I didn't like the product I was

representing," Scheff says today. "I didn't want to go to work for IBM and that seemed the only alternative if I stayed in word-processing. You just can't worry about people picking on you and saying, 'Hey, you're crazy to do this.' My wife said it, my lawyer said it, my accountant said it." Scheff knew he must go ahead and he knew he would succeed by the power of his will. "I had," he says, "a great desire not to fail."

But before CPT could finish development of its Model 4200, the young corporation saw its resources dwindling dangerously low. Furthermore, there were flaws in the prototype. Simply put, Scheff and his cohorts couldn't get the device to run reliably. Norman Flaaten remembers a phone conversation: "We couldn't get the machine running," he says, "and we couldn't get the funding we needed. Dean said, 'I'm flipping a coin, wondering if we should have a party with the money we have left before closing our doors.' Then, all of a sudden, things broke loose. We got our piece of hardware to work, we got our exposure, and we landed our funding. It seemed like a miraculous chain of events." Midland, a small securities firm, took CPT public in December 1971, and in that offering CPT raised $500,000 in new capital—enough to finish the 4200 and ship the first orders in June 1972.

CPT sold 166,667 shares of common stock at $3 per share in that initial offering. Scheff braced himself and kept on marching. With the introduction of the CPT-4200, the stock rose from $3 to $6 in three months.

Just as in the old days of the "Dick and Dean Show," Eichhorn and Scheff teamed up in a Minneapolis skyway to pitch the CPT-4200. The pair demonstrated two units and took some 30 orders in a single day. Secretaries, watching the show, were immediately enthusiastic. They coaxed their bosses out to see the 4200 in action.

"The adrenalin was pumping," says Jim Weinhold, "and after that debut on the skyway, it really started to pump. Those two came back to CPT like kids with a new toy."

CPT sales people, asked so often to explain the acronym, were supplied with a list of word combinations starting with the three letters. "Call it what you want," a marketing executive quipped. "IBM calls us that 'Cotton Pickin' Thing.' "

CPT, meanwhile, launched a newspaper advertising campaign aimed at a punchy comparison:

"How can a little company from Minnesota compete with the giants from New York?" the ad said.

"A better product," it said. "A better price."

Simple as that.

Well, maybe not so simple. Scheff's well-developed dealer network began reporting in. Some potential buyers thought CPT's comparatively low price was suspicious. If the CPT-4200 costs only half as much as the IBM model, they said, it might be only half as good. Some companies, one dealer said, "wouldn't even let us in the door. They wanted the assurance that our product would do the job, that the service support was there, that the company wasn't going to go out of business. So they would deal only with IBM."

Scheff took a close look at his market. Most of his sales were one or two CPT-4200s to small firms in small communities. Thus, he would concentrate on those buyers until CPT built up its inventory, its reputation and its marketing savvy. *Then* Scheff would challenge IBM head-on. "To paraphrase Chairman Mao," Scheff told a business reporter, "I believe that if the countryside falls, the cities will follow."

CPT's total sales reached $73,000 in fiscal 1972. The company moved out of its bingo parlor and into 16,000 respectable square feet in the suburbs. In 1973, sales rose to $2 million, and, in 1974, to $6.6 million. By 1977, that $6.6-million sales figure had doubled. By 1978, it had been tripled, and, by 1980, it had been multiplied eight-and-a-half times.

Scheff and his CPT colleagues were continually adding refinements to the word-processing design during that period, and, in 1977, they introduced the CPT 8000, a second-generation model. The 8000 was not just a super-typewriter and a cassette tape, but a high-speed printer with an easy-to-read black-on-white display screen, a microprocessor and a memory. It was a device that, depending on the program, could "speak" in 17 languages including Arabic, handle thorny mathematical calculations and even answer points of law, thanks to West Publishing's Westlaw software. And, realizing that CPT should not be just a manufacturer of machinery, Scheff moved the company into the development of its own software series called WordPak. The software, introduced in 1979, permits a typist to recall, sift through and manipulate information on the screen. Like other manufacturers of word-processing hardware, Scheff could see the importance of both hard- and software economics. No one wishing to remain competitive could afford to ignore either facet of the twin consumer need.

In 1979, CPT introduced the Model 6000, which was capable of filling the void between the entry-level 4200 and the "super-brain" 8000. And, in 1981, the company brought out the 8100 and 6100 word processors, with 50 and 33 percent more memory, respectively, than their predecessors. Strategically, Scheff was covering all the bases.

□ Just a decade after its origin, Dean Scheff announced that CPT Corporation would have sales exceeding $100 million annually and that by the mid-1980s that figure would rise to $500 million. An original share that sold for $3 in 1971 was worth $300 in February 1982. He was, moreover, looking at a worldwide word-processing market with stunning possibilities. Only 10 percent of that market, he said, had been tapped.

In the past 10 years, CPT has extracted its price from Scheff, but all along he's seemed eager to pay it. From the beginning, says Dick Eichhorn, Scheff has worked 11- and 12-hour days. "He thoroughly enjoys working when the enterprise is his baby. That's how he perceives CPT. Dean has virtually no life outside CPT. His wife works for the corporation as an interior-design consultant. He has not spent much time with his children, but he has no apparent regrets about that. Dean's work habits have not changed since 1971."

When Eichhorn, himself planning an early retirement, broached the subject of succession and retirement to Scheff recently, Scheff balked. "Dean wanted no part of it," Eichhorn says. "When I began to think about my own retirement, it seemed that one of the best things I could do was help Dean start thinking about his own. Dean had garnered all the income, all the prestige, all the respect he needed. I approached him a couple times, but I could see it was hopeless. 'It's my baby,' he was saying to me. 'I can't give it up.' Dean will lead the parade at CPT until he's carried out."

"I can't retire yet," Scheff, now in his early 50s, says simply. "I get bored too easily."

What is it that drives Dean Scheff? The answers vary.

"The challenge of succeeding at a difficult task against gigantic competition," says John MacLennan. "Money is not so important. He has more than he can spend."

"Power in the purest sense," says Eichhorn. "Not that he uses it. He just wants to know he has it."

"Psychic success," says Scheff himself. "More than the external trappings."

Eichhorn believes that Scheff trusts no one with CPT but himself. When Scheff does delegate, events in CPT's life suggest that he will not trust fully or for long. In 1977, Scheff hired two men new to the industry and elevated them both to senior vice presidencies. One took charge of CPT sales and marketing; the other was given responsibility for engineering and production. "They had the power to make or break CPT," Eichhorn says. "Dean let them have the freedom to work. But, in a short time, both had made enough bad decisions, so Dean climbed back on top."

The new senior VPs lasted two years. "It was bad chemistry from the start," Scheff told a reporter. "After I turned responsibility over to them, things just seemed to get worse. From minimal structure at CPT we went to absolute chaos overnight—from halfway decent to utter pits."

In addition, both men were apparently vying to succeed Scheff as president, and he would have none of that. "Years ago, I assured Dean that I *didn't* want to be president," Dick Eichhorn says. "When he finally came to believe that, he was comfortable with me." The jockeying of the senior vice presidents, Eichhorn says, was more than a little discomfiting to Scheff.

□ The trust issue surfaced again in January 1982. In 1980, Scheff had relinquished day-to-day operations to Gary Holland, a young professional manager from the Toro Company. Scheff did it, insiders say, because his board put pressure on him to hire a man like Holland who could address CPT's inevitable growing pains. By 1980, Dick Eichhorn says, CPT was understaffed and lacking sufficient structure. Quality control had suffered, and the company needed more orderly, effective procedures for billing, bill-paying, parts-shipping and inventory control. In its race to keep apace of market demands, no one seemed to have much time for strategic planning or performance evaluation.

"A mess of a company," one CPT insider told a reporter. In some ways, the CPT of 1980 reflected Scheff's disregard for system and formality. In classic entrepreneurial fashion, Scheff was the pragmatic, seat-of-the-pants operator. Reluctant to delegate, impatient with chains of command. A man given to unilateral decision-making, not team-building.

But Scheff did give Gary Holland unparalleled responsibility in 1980, and this time the new man didn't fail him. In about a year, Holland successfully restructured CPT along 10 functional lines, each with its own vice president. He added staff and built management teams, and everyone reported to him except Dale Clift, vice president of finance. Holland instituted important new controls in accounting, marketing, sales and production. New quality programs weeded out defective incoming parts and outgoing CPT products. CPT started 1982 with annual revenues up 71 percent and shareholder equity up 61 percent. Forecasts pegged CPT's growth rate for 1982 at 50 percent.

Gary Holland's future seemed secure. The CPT staff and dealer network respected him. He was winning kudos. Then, in January, Scheff returned from a vacation and dismissed him.

"Dean was getting less recognition, and more was falling to other people," says Dick Eichhorn. "I think Dean realized that he wasn't ready to give up CPT. 'I need this,' he seemed to be saying, 'I have to come back and be the central figure.'" Eichhorn also theorizes that Scheff considered the CPT growing pains a reflection on his own ability to lead and manage. "I think Dean felt he had to go back and erase that black mark from his record," Eichhorn says. "It's not an issue on the street, but it is with him."

Robert Knutson, a CPT board member since the company's beginning, offered another explanation to a business reporter. "A company is like a country," Knutson said, not long after Holland's departure. "CPT is run by a dictator, and a dictator has to have a purge every once in a while.... This is the fourth major purge at CPT that I can remember, and there have been other smaller ones. I don't think Scheff is the kind of person who can have a president under him. No matter how big that company gets, he has to be the boss."

Dean Scheff's management style is simply not given to teamwork. He is outspoken, he is single-minded, he is tough on people who err. "He cannot stand incompetence," says Eichhorn. "He likes to play the devil's advocate, and he rejects 'yes' men. He believes in kick-'em-in-the-ass management. He will mercilessly go after people in front of others. People who stay at CPT learn to live with it.

"As the company grew," Eichhorn continues, "I saw Dean change. As CPT became more complex and Dean couldn't keep his fingers in every pie, he became more cantankerous."

"Scheff is the best user of people I've ever seen in my life," a former CPT employee said recently. "He tries to run the company on fear, and he gets maximum output from people because of it. If you're not producing, he knows it." The same man, however, said he would work for Scheff again "in a minute." "I'm a successful businessman now," he says, "and a lot of things I learned from Scheff are responsible for that."

How does Scheff describe his management style? In a word, "mean." "I consider myself," he says, "very demanding."

Demanding *and* unorthodox may be descriptive of his entrepreneurial style as well: "I'm not sure the entrepreneur fits well in society," he says. "He has some resentment of authority. He won't go to work for anyone. He is virtually unemployable. He knows he's smarter and better than anyone who would hire him."

Dean Scheff has been smart enough to maintain increasing profits during CPT's costly, risky formative years. He's been smart enough to listen keenly to whispers in the marketplace and respond quickly to subtle shifts in demand. He's been smart enough to find his niche in an industry dominated by the high and the mighty.

Perhaps he's *not* smart enough to let CPT grow beyond his singular influence, some say. But the jury is still out in that case. As far as Scheff is concerned, it is a jury of one.

Curt Carlson

12

Curt Carlson

Stamped in Gold

"All I want," the 22-year-old Curt Carlson told his job-hungry classmates, "is the freedom that comes with a regular income." No commission sales job. No cash-poor company. No uncertainty.

Who could blame him? Like everybody else in Depression-weary Minnesota, Carlson had to scrape to pay his college tuition. He delivered groceries, stacked cases of soda pop, hustled newspapers, worked every job he could find to finance four years at the University of Minnesota. Now he was ready to graduate, to begin earning a decent living and to marry the blonde he met in his political science class.

More than anything else, Carlson wanted stability, and Procter & Gamble made the best offer—$110 a month to sell soap and shortening to grocery stores in south Minneapolis. He already knew the territory, since he'd grown up there. He also knew the grocery business, since his father had spent the better part of his life peddling goods to those same grocery stores. Selling, in fact, came naturally to a Carlson.

So beginning in June 1937, Curt Carlson promoted Crisco, Oxydol, Camay, Ivory, Kirk's Castile and Dreft with evangelistic fervor. He soon collided with arch-competitors Lever Brothers and Colgate, and discovered, to his surprise, that P & G was no favorite among South Side grocers. He learned that P & G sales people were urged to push hard.

"Aggressive exploitation," P & G called it. Push for more shelf-space in each store. Push for more inventory. Load grocers up with Oxydol and Dreft. Paper their windows with promotion banners. Crowd their aisles with "shelf-talkers." Pack in 15 calls a day to 15 grocers. Don't waste your time with congenial small talk. When a grocer resists, go back at him again. And again. Don't let up. Don't lose heart. Don't take the rejections personally. This is guerilla warfare.

Carlson learned to stiffen his backbone. He learned to even threaten: "You don't buy from me? I'll take my Oxydol and my specials to your competition...." Carlson's canny commander at P & G urged him on. "If you don't get thrown out of at least one grocery store a week," C.W. Mussett growled, "you're not selling hard enough."

Mussett's gritty pragmatism appealed to Carlson, who was raised on long work days and discipline. On his own, he had learned that there was more than one way to make a sale and that the successful peddler was the one who didn't give up too soon. And, at 23, Carlson sold more soap than any other P & G man in Minnesota, Iowa, Wisconsin, Montana and the Dakotas. For his precocious success at "aggressive exploitation," the rookie salesman won a dress watch and $330.

That was nice, Carlson decided, but not nice enough. The young man with a mind for minutiae—especially financial minutiae—started figuring. His efforts were worth more than a dress watch and $330. "It would have meant thousands had I been working for myself," he scoffed. *"Hundreds* of thousands."

Curt Carlson's dissatisfaction with a steady, secure income working for somebody else began the day he won the watch. It was that dissatisfaction that made him start his own company just 12 months after he signed on with P & G. It was that dissatisfaction that empowered him to build a company that is today one of America's 14 largest

privately held corporations, with annual sales approaching
$2 billion.

☐ Anyone watching Curtis Leroy Carlson grow up would
have seen a kid with bold ventures in his eyes. Carlson had
spotted money-making schemes and had people working
for him before most kids set up their first lemonade stand.

"If you can get a dozen new customers to take the *Minneapolis Journal*, you can have the route," a local route
manager challenged Carlson in 1924. "I'm making the
same offer to the current carrier." Armed with a list of
prospects, Carlson made his pitch and quickly came back
with a dozen new orders, while his competition had none.
That first paper route paid him $15 a month, which wasn't
bad for a 10-year-old in those days. Furthermore, he could
keep all his earnings. While many other kids with jobs had
to pay their room and board, the children of Charles
Carlson, a wholesale food broker, could keep everything
they made. The arrangement gave Curt the incentive to
make more.

"Let me take over another route," he said to his route
manager. "I'll find you more customers." The second successful route gave rise to a third, and Carlson became the
only *Journal* carrier with multiple routes. He drafted his
brothers and sister to work for him, and, though only the
third-born of the five children, he orchestrated the entire
operation. He had learned, among other things, that replication was a good thing; that if one paper route made $15 a
month, three could triple that amount. He also learned
about control, and that the one to profit most was the one
who was in charge. He would learn about economies of
scale later.

There were other youthful ventures besides paper routes:
shoveling snow, mowing lawns, selling lemonade and but-
termilk. Summer mornings, Carlson dragged himself out
of bed at 4:30 and caught a pre-dawn streetcar to Interlachen Country Club. He would place his name near the
top of the caddies' list and then head back home to deliver
his morning papers. When he finished his route, he returned to Interlachen for the morning's first 18-hole
round. When Carlson considered skipping a day at Interlachen, his mother would deliver a homily on responsibility.

Why shouldn't Curt embrace the work ethic? His father routinely worked 12-hour days selling and servicing local groceries. He left home early, came back late and earned a good living. And, as if running a household and raising five children wasn't enough, Carlson's mother opened a bakery. The Carlson family wasn't desperate for a second income, but Mrs. Carlson thrived on work. She also wanted a bank account of her own. The messages, then, were loud and clear—work hard, keep commitments, manage your money, don't ask for handouts, never give up.

Curt Carlson learned to draw from his own well. By the time he was in high school, thousands of Minnesotans were out of work and there was little hope for a summer job. One day, riding in an elevator after being turned down for work by General Mills, the affable Carlson struck up a conversation with a young man about five years older than he was.

"Did you just come from the employment agency upstairs?" Carlson asked.

"Yup," the young man said brightly. "Gave me two prospects."

"Good for you," said Carlson. "What are they?"

"Bellhop at Farmers & Mechanics paying $45 a month and a clerk at the Grain Exchange paying $55."

"Which one you going after?" Carlson inquired.

"The Exchange," said the young man.

Carlson bid the job hunter good-by and headed for F & M. "I'm here about a job," he said, and he got it. No one ever asked if he was sent by the employment agency.

"A person needs the fear of being out of a job," Carlson would tell a reporter later. "In the 1930s, you had to figure out a way to get a buck...or you never got one."

Pragmatism wedded with the work ethic made Curt Carlson formidable. He could keep his newspaper empire active *and* pull in a tidy sum from F & M. At the time, it seems, Carlson had his eye on a blue Chevrolet convertible—quite the status symbol for anyone, let alone a high school kid, in the depths of the Depression. So when F & M invited him to work past summer vacation, he put school aside.

"You *have* to finish high school," his mother said, imagining him in a law firm one day.

"I will," he promised. "I'll work just long enough to buy that car."

He negotiated with his West High School advisor so he could skip routine classes, yet graduate the following year with his own class. As things turned out, he got both his degree and the Chevy convertible.

Achievement had always figured prominently in the Carlson household, and it was not out of disrespect that young Curt wanted to achieve more than his father had. Charles Carlson was raised on a farm near North Branch, Minnesota. He had a third-grade education and worked for others as a salesman most of his adult life. Not until "retirement" did Charles Carlson embark on a couple of business ventures of his own. And when he died, he left the family about $300,000.

Curt Carlson would graduate from the University of Minnesota with a bachelor's degree in economics, start his own "adult" business at 23 with $50, and build his net worth to more than $100 million by 1981. He would learn to act on the lessons of his youth, and he would achieve things that other men only dream about.

□ Procter & Gamble gave Curt Carlson the education he never got in his four years at the university. His career with P & G would have lasted longer, too, were it not for three things: the wrist watch, the red tape associated with selling for a giant company—and the yellowed, 20-year-old trading-stamp book he found tucked away in his in-laws' buffet.

The book reminded Carlson of buying Christmas presents at Leader's Department Store in downtown Minneapolis. Leader's gave one Red Security Stamp for every 10 cents of purchase. Fill up a book, the clerk told him, and turn it in for cash. Leader's hadn't been the first to use stamps, Carlson would learn. Nearly 50 years earlier, Schuster's Department Store in Milwaukee had introduced stamps as an inducement to buy at its store.

Carlson looked at the little book and started scheming. If stamps drew customers to department stores, why wouldn't they lure shoppers to grocery stores? Stamps made even more sense for grocers, he thought. What sets one grocer apart from the others when everyone carries essentially the same products? Grocery stores represented an obvious untapped market, and one he could reach. He understood the grocer's mentality; he grew up with it. And with the kind of promotional blitz he'd learned from P & G, he and his grocers could make the consumer crazy for the stamps.

He talked about the idea to people close to him. His erstwhile economics professor at the university discouraged him. So did a local banker. So did Carlson's parents. The jury delivering a near-unanimous "don't do it" included his wife, Arleen, who was pregnant with their first child. It was too risky, they said. How would he support his family? The Depression was still sucking the life out of Minnesota. But Carlson had what he now calls "restless genes." He was a maverick, and the jury couldn't dissuade him.

Only Arleen Carlson's father, Charles Martin, supported the young man's decision. Martin understood his son-in-law's entrepreneurial instincts: Martin, after all, owned and ran his own business. In fact, in 1938, when Carlson was itching to leave the security of Procter & Gamble, Charles Martin's Kladezee clothing store on Nicollet Avenue represented another career option.

Carlson borrowed $50 to get started. He named his new stamp "Gold Bond" (gold for value, bond for safety), registered his company with the state of Minnesota and set up shop. The date was June 8, 1938, and the Gold Bond Stamp Company was a mail drop and desk space in the Plymouth Building in downtown Minneapolis. He paid a secretary working for somebody else $5 a month to answer the Gold Bond phone.

But Carlson, aware of the risks, didn't leave Procter & Gamble immediately. Burning the bridge too soon seemed foolish. No, he would continue peddling Crisco and Oxydol during the day and devote his evenings and weekends to persuading one grocer after another to try trading stamps. Years later, when his own salesmen told him Saturday was a tough day to sell, he would set them straight: *"Every* day is a tough day to sell. If you work five days a week, all you do is stay even with the competition. The sixth day—that's the day you get ahead."

Carlson had to use all the salesmanship he could muster on those small grocers. The Depression had eroded their incomes, so it was especially hard for them to accept the idea of surrendering two percent of the gross to Gold Bond for the stamp program. Even if Carlson promised a 20 percent increase in sales for that two percent investment, many grocers still turned him down. But rejection was not a new experience for any P & G salesman. Carlson would go back again and again, never giving up, never losing heart.

Nine months after Gold Bond's creation, Carlson made his first sale—to Anfin Odland Grocers on 12th Avenue South in Minneapolis. Carlson gave Odland the exclusive right to dispense and redeem Gold Bond stamps in a 25-block area. That first stamp order totaled $14.50. If all those stamps were redeemed for cash, Carlson would pay out no more than $10. Research by older and wiser stamp companies, however, told Carlson that about five percent of all stamps given out are never redeemed.

Odland's modest order was certainly not in scale with Carlson's unbridled delight that day in March 1939. GRAND OPENING, a banner shouted. WE GIVE GOLD BOND STAMPS, another sign declared. There were posters in the windows and on the walls, plus balloons and refreshments. Carlson had unleashed his promoter's flair with the help of a 35-cent-an-hour sign painter.

Carlson had driven his wife to Odland's store the night before the grand opening. Like a thief who was casing the joint, Carlson pressed his face to Odland's front window and turned his flashlight on the display inside. What he saw was the potential for replication that went far beyond three newspaper routes. "If it works here," he told Arleen, "there are *hundreds* of grocers who will buy our stamps."

☐ Eighteen months into his new business, Curt Carlson paused to assess his double life. He was pulling in $150 a month plus bonuses for record sales from Procter & Gamble. His Gold Bond Stamp Company had landed a grand total of 40 grocery accounts. "You can't play it safe," he told a friend. "A person can't be too cautious and be an entrepreneur. You just have to jump in. If things don't turn out right, then you make them right by taking another run at it. Entrepreneurs dig holes and climb out." He said good-by to Procter & Gamble.

Carlson moved his company to 106 South 11th Street in Minneapolis, next door to a Chinese restaurant and a pinball machine-servicing outfit. He then asked Joe Hunt, a junior clerk at the U.S. Department of Agriculture office in St. Paul, to share the new space and coat closet. Hunt was to be the "inside man," servicing accounts, even firing up the nearby furnace to burn redeemed stamps. Carlson would be the "outside man," making pitch upon pitch to unsold grocers.

Carlson at that point inaugurated what would become a personal ritual. He set his first business goal—to earn $100 a week—and wrote it on a slip of paper and tucked it in his wallet. He would look at that slip of paper regularly and consider his progress. Until he began making that $100 a week, the white flag in his billfold would drive him on.

In the meantime, Arleen Carlson reluctantly donned a golden majorette's costume and feathered headband for her husband's grocery store promotions. After a grand entrance, Carlson positioned Arleen at a cardtable near the door where she could beckon shoppers as they came in. In her quiet style, she told homemakers how easy it was to save stamps and redeem them for cash.

But though business looked promising, Carlson had a cash-flow problem. He had to finance those stamp promotions before he realized any income from the new grocers joining the program. To cover the gap, he went to First National Bank of Minneapolis for a $1,000 loan. Yet even with signed contracts in hand, he was turned down.

When further cash-flow troubles threatened Gold Bond's solvency in 1940, Carlson sold a half-dozen $100 shares to a handful of friends. But he bought those shares back as soon as he could, for he had no intention of selling off parts of his company and losing control. Finally, in 1941, Carlson had some 200 grocery accounts in the Twin Cities and nearby towns. Things were just beginning to look up for Gold Bond when Japanese planes bombed Pearl Harbor. Three months later, Gold Bond had lost two-thirds of its business. What grocer needed trading stamps in wartime? If he had food on his shelves in that era of shortages, people flocked to his store with their ration books. The draw was scarce food, not stamps.

Carlson would wait this out. He believed in the stamp concept, and when the war ended, he'd be ready. Meanwhile, he kept his skeletal Gold Bond operation going and doubled as sales manager for Charles Martin's clothing store.

Carlson's two employees, Joe Hunt and Alvina Lenzen, Gold Bond's secretary, both joined the service. When Carlson was classified 1-A, he went to the Navy, which offered him ensign status. In what may have been a first for the Navy, the 27-year-old Swede from south Minneapolis said he would settle for no less than lieutenant j.g. The young man was a good salesman, the officers agreed, but not good enough. Carlson went home and waited for his draft notice and wondered who would run Gold Bond when he was called up.

Eventually, he looked to Truman Johnson, a Procter & Gamble executive in Wisconsin. The two had talked about the stamp business. Just before the war broke out, during a dining-room conversation at what would later become one of Carlson's hotels (the downtown Radisson), Carlson had even asked Johnson to join him. Johnson put $5 in earnest money toward the pact. But time passed, the war intervened, and it was not until 1944 that Johnson and Carlson finally made a deal.

The terms were tough—Johnson wanted half interest in Gold Bond. As it happened, it would be the last time Carlson gave up a chunk of his enterprise—and its leadership—to anyone. Shared command didn't suit him. Nor, for that matter, would he ever go public and submit his enterprise to the scrutiny of shareholders and the Securities and Exchange Commission. That would mean giving up ultimate control—and the flexibility to act quickly. But in 1944, Carlson needed a cohort to manage Gold Bond and he trusted the man who'd been modeled by P & G.

Over the next 14 years, until Carlson finally bought Johnson out, he, Johnson and Joe Hunt would be critically aware of the ownership ties that united them. Carlson owned 48 percent; Johnson, 48, and Hunt, two. The relationship often felt like a deadlock.

After the war, Carlson, Johnson and Hunt were busy regaining business for Gold Bond. They hired Vernon McCoy, a savvy wholesale food salesman from Stokely Van Camp, to work Wisconsin and open up new territories in Texas, Indiana and Oregon. Carlson's replication theory was a natural for trading stamps. Why stop with independent grocers? Why not service stations and drycleaners? In addition, McCoy sold stamps to movie theaters, feed and grain millers, even undertakers and a turkey hatchery.

A student of statistics, McCoy researched the cost of doing business for each enterprise and plotted the various margins and breakeven points. Thus, he could pitch Gold Bond's two percent investment for a 20 percent sales gain with compelling accuracy. Carlson and his company did their homework. Golden days returned to Gold Bond.

In 1946, Carlson and Johnson developed a five-year program. Gold Bond would expand its operations into seven states. Carlson even coined a slogan: "It Shall Be Done in '51." Facets of that plan found their way into Carlson's wallet on slips of "goal paper." Both men agreed that the real plum would be grocery chains. National Tea openly opposed stamps at the time. Red Owl and Super Valu straddled the fence, but they were interested enough to make inquiries. Red Owl offered to pay Gold Bond one percent of its gross for the stamps, not the customary two. Super Valu, for its part, wanted customers to redeem stamps for premiums rather than cash.

The big breakthrough came in April 1953—Super Valu stores in Minneapolis began offering Gold Bond stamps. The trading stamp industry, including arch-rival S & H, snapped to attention. Carlson's instinct for replication and promotion had garnered the first American chain grocer. Ads covered multiple pages in the local newspapers. Mailers and radio spots announced the Gold Bond debut and offered free stamps and the promise of gifts. Super Valu stores were jammed.

Carlson and Johnson struggled to accommodate the shift from cash to premiums. Super Valu's demand meant that Gold Bond needed warehouses and inventory, redemption centers and people to staff them. It was all new territory, and if there was a slogan for the era it was "Do and Learn."

☐ The 1950s invited risk-taking, and Kroger stores provided the biggest risk of all. Kroger, the giant food chain, was ready to offer stamps. Cappel-MacDonald, a major premium supplier, called Carlson. "If you can handle the stamps for Kroger, we'll handle the premiums," the supplier said.

Super Valu, not surprisingly, objected to Kroger offering Gold Bond Stamps, so Carlson, unwilling to miss the giant opportunity, suggested that Gold Bond create *another* stamp company to serve Kroger. The idea could mean $1 billion in business over the next several years, not to mention an enormous expansion in territory. Carlson was beginning to see just how large his enterprise could grow. The Kroger opportunity posed one big risk, however, for this modest Midwestern company with only 225 employees. If Carlson figured wrong on any facet of staffing, supply or cost, the Kroger deal could bankrupt Gold Bond.

Risk notwithstanding, Curt Carlson was ready to go ahead. But Truman Johnson wavered. If there was one subject that underscored their differences, the Kroger deal was it. Johnson was content to see Gold Bond live within its means, following a conservative, slow—but steady—growth route. Take only small to moderate risks, he counseled. Carlson prevailed, however, and the Kroger deal was consummated.

In fact, seeing the increasing value of stamps, Carlson decided to go after other, non-competitive chains with the new Top Value stamp program. Stop & Shop in Boston, Hart's in upstate New York, Penn Fruit in Philadelphia, Humpty Dumpty in Oklahoma, Hinky Dinky in Omaha. The return for Carlson and his company was multiplying fast. All he had to do was hire and train 300 new salesmen to sell those new territories and service the member grocery chains. But that meant more than doubling his staff, and he was suddenly struck by the magnitude of that assignment.

"You know," he told a biographer later, "a fellow doesn't have to be the smartest man in the world to be a success. But he does have to have the guts to hang in there when things get tough. And he's got to be able to figure with a pencil. You can misspell and get away with it, but if you misfigure, you won't last long."

Carlson was not one to misfigure. About one year into the Top Value stamp program, Kroger lobbied to buy Carlson's share in the enterprise. Carlson didn't want out, but Kroger pressed hard in every way it knew how. The eventual sale of Gold Bond's Top Value interest, in 1957, brought a cool $1 million in cash to Carlson and Johnson —which was enough, Carlson thought, to end the partnership.

Carlson offered to buy Johnson out—or to sell out to him—depending on the price they determined for Gold Bond. Carlson told Johnson he had no intention of leaving the stamp business. If he sold his interest to Johnson, Carlson would start another stamp company in the next, most promising market, California, then gradually work his way east. Before long, Carlson cautioned, the two of them would be competitors. Carlson was in the stamp business to stay. Johnson admitted he was not; he would take an early retirement if he sold his share of the business. Carlson prevailed. He bought out Johnson for $1 million and $50,000 a year for the next five years. Carlson would once again grow at the pace and in the direction only *he* decided.

In the years that followed, Carlson and his Gold Bond staff brought Safeway Stores of Oakland, California, into the fold. Carlson dispatched salesmen and promotional teams to new territories with the intensity of a blitzkrieg (his ablest strategists and advance men chosen to descend on target areas were nicknamed "the Flying Squadron"). Carlson also expanded into Canada, the Caribbean, Japan and several other countries around the world.

But by the early 1960s, American consumers were beginning to seek discounted prices, not premiums. They blamed trading stamps for raising the price of their goods. Carlson fought those anti-stamp sentiments with lobbyists of his own. He even found a legislative friend in Hubert Humphrey. Carlson lost Safeway Stores in this wave of anti-stamp feeling, but he countered by picking up another large chain, Bayless. It was clear by that time, however, that the popularity of trading stamps was waning.

"We're going to fight back," Carlson told his staff. "If a major account gives us notice, we'll fight back with everything we've got. We're going to make it damn expensive when they quit." In the spirit of blitzkriegs past, the Gold Bond crew won many stores back and turned Gold Bond's initial loss into a modest gain. But Carlson could see that stamps were on an inevitable decline. Now the blitz was only a delaying tactic. He would have to decide when and how to deal with the trend.

Carlson's answer was diversification and acquisition. He moved his company into hotels and restaurants, into catalog showrooms and real estate and manufacturing. He picked businesses where he could apply his promotional savvy and businesses that fit his replication strategy. The "cash cows," as Carlson called them—ventures that resisted replication—would not be part of the empire. Nor would ventures that depended heavily on external variables like fluctuating interest rates and gold prices. Those factors were beyond even Carlson's control.

Carlson picked businesses he could build from within. Never enter a business you know little about—unless you can buy the talent to run it, he would tell his troops. Or he would acquire tidy operations and swiftly take them private. The private posture was always important. While a publicly traded company busied itself assembling its board of directors to draft an acquisition offer, Carlson was already en route to the target company's door—offer in hand. Over time, that flexibility allowed Carlson to pick up a number of attractive morsels in the marketplace.

☐ Curt Carlson has always had a firm grip on the reins of his company, and, though now in his late 60s, he still holds them tight. The man still demands much of himself and the people around him. Indeed, some say *too* much. For many years, 10 hours a day, six days a week was Carlson's expectation for himself and his staff. He still works an occasional Saturday, though the need no longer exists.

Executives who perform well can bask in the gifting and paternalism that emanates from Curt Carlson's lordly suite at Carlson Companies' world headquarters in Plymouth. Top performers earn as much as 50 percent of their annual take-home pay in bonuses. They drive Lincoln Continentals, wear diamond-studded rings and travel around the world, free of charge, with their boss. Carlson, the entrepreneur, believes in a big reward for a big effort. On the other hand, a lackluster performer can often bring down the vocal rage of the chief. "The worst thing he can call you is a 'rank amateur,' " says one insider. "Then you know that you're through."

Carlson admits little, if any, self-doubt. When he fails—and he has—he simply tries another tack. He is single-minded and willful. "An entrepreneur has to have supreme confidence," he says. "I can't doubt myself." His objective is to remain, he says, "unconfused." "All we do is keep our eye on the target," Carlson told his biographer. "Obstacles are those frightening things you see when you take your eye off the target."

Carlson has borrowed heavily, risked much, built big ("size gives you clout"). "You don't see good entrepreneurs shooting craps," he says, "but you do see them relying on their intuition. Entrepreneurs have a high hurdle rate. After looking at all the facts available, the hurdle is the unknown between me and the decision. I can't analyze things to death. Lawyers and accountants do that. I have to take the hurdles and rely on my own instincts. I have to make the jump. If it doesn't turn out right, I have to make it right."

Part of Carlson's determination was no doubt born of the Depression. "Growing up and building a business during that time," he says, "I always had fear behind me ...and a carrot in front of me. The environment shapes a person's resolve. If I'd had it too easy in my earlier life, I may have given up when things got tough."

What drives Curt Carlson? Power, close associates say. Power and achievement. Outdoing his father. Surpassing his own goals. The money he makes, Carlson insists, is not the ultimate reward, only the measurement of his achievement.

Carlson has spent that money on a $3-million home liberally decorated with antiques and statuary. His two daughters and their families live beside him in what could be called the Carlson Compound, perched on a hill overlooking a quiet bay of Lake Minnetonka. He has an 85-foot yacht, the *Curt-C*, which he keeps in Minnesota during the summer and in Florida during the winter. North of the Twin Cities, on Lake Minnesuing, he's converted a modest cottage that's been in his family for some 70 years into a multi-building retreat complete with stables, swimming pool, bowling alley and golf course. Minnesuing is the site of both family and corporate gatherings, where, in all cases, Carlson is the patriarch.

In Twin Cities social circles, however, Curt Carlson is sometimes considered *nouveau riche*, a bit rough around the edges, and not fully acceptable to some of the older wealthy families of the region. Prestige is important to him, a close friend says. He wants that acceptance in his own community, and he goes out of his way to serve on local fund-raising committees and civic-improvement projects. He is much decorated (Swedish-American of the Year, Minnesotan of the Year, a member of the Minnesota Business Hall of Fame and a Horatio Alger Award winner) and takes easily and eagerly to the spotlight. "Look," says close friend and co-worker John Heim, "a wild-eyed, aggressively promotional stamp company is not highly regarded for its very nature, so it's been important to Curt to gain local legitimacy. He expected his family to grow up and live here after him. He was going to fix it for his family. He wants his company and family to have stature." Already, it appears, Carlson's daughters have been accepted more readily into "polite society" than their father ever was.

No one close to Curt Carlson really believes he will ever retire. He is grooming a son-in-law, Edwin C. Gage, to follow him, many say, but as long as he occupies company headquarters on Highway 55 he will be the boss. For the time being, there is work to be done, new ventures to entertain.

"You know," he says, "one of the advantages of getting bigger is that everyone hustles you to go in with them or to back them." He clearly enjoys the attention. And that's how Curtis Homes joined the Carlson Companies two years ago. The founder of the company, whose son was running it, came to Carlson: "I'll supply the capital," the father said, "but I want him to work for *you*." "Now Curtis Homes is going like wildfire," Carlson beams, "even in what experts call a housing slump. Our homes are the basic shell with the roof and heavy wiring installed. The homeowner does the rest—floors, paneling, woodwork. Here's a chance to get into a beautiful home for $60,000. No big dollar investment, just a lot of sweat equity."

"Sweat equity." It's obviously a concept Curt Carlson can endorse. He built his own empire on it.